COUNTRYSIDE AND CLOISTER

*Reminiscences of
a Carmelite Nun*

Marie T Litchfield

FAMILY PUBLICATIONS

COUNTRYSIDE & CLOISTER

Reminiscences of a Carmelite Nun

by Marie T Litchfield

© Family Publications, 1997

ISBN 1 871217 23 7

cover design by

Joanna Pitt

line drawings by

Rosemary Roberts

published by

FAMILY PUBLICATIONS

77 Banbury Road, Oxford OX2 6LF

Tel: 01865 514408   *Fax:* 01865 552774

printed by

The Cromwell Press, Trowbridge, Wilts

Contents

Foreword

'There is nothing but poetry about the existence of childhood, real simple soul-moving poetry, the laughter and joy of poetry and not its philosophy'. John Clare might have continued – and happy are those who while searching for universal truths are still able to hold on to some of the poetical sunshine of childhood to illuminate their lives thereafter.

Anyone who reads a book – any book – should, to gain full benefit from the exercise, enjoy a one-to-one encounter with the author. They would in a very real way experience a further level of consciousness in that the episodes described on the printed page become vividly their own.

Countryside & Cloister expresses a love for others and a satisfaction with a chosen way of life that, in a world where such feelings are seldom felt let alone given voice to, the reminiscences of Sister Marie, reflecting as they do her love of people and joy in the simple things God has given us, had me smiling at the reality of a shared pleasure.

Richard Jefferies, an author whose works I read in my teenage years, influenced my life afterwards to a modest degree. A book on the life of St Thérèse of Lisieux, read when she was a little girl, had so profound an influence on Marie Litchfield that it set the guidelines for the whole of her career. To devote her life to the utmost for God and the good of people everywhere became her stated ambition. Reading the book will reveal just how completely and happily the author accomplished this. The days that absorb the soul and fill the mind with beauty signify a real God-reflecting life and, surely, all else is mere endurance.

Like Sister Marie may we all take our delight in the simple things which in a busy world are so easily overlooked. Reading *Countryside & Cloister* will be one step along a happier road for those who care to make the journey with the author through childhood to where the reader shares her delight in a solitary clump of sorrel growing beside a hawthorn hedge. A gem of a book, and reading it was to me a mind-enriching experience.

Geoffrey Smith
October 1997

For my family and Community, in gratitude.

Preface

These reminiscences started out as jottings for my brothers and sisters and for their children and grandchildren. They in no way set out to be a life story. Rather they are glimpses of nature, people and landscapes from my childhood in Somerset, and since in monasteries in Devonshire and Yorkshire.

I hope that they will evoke memories and interest in village and family life of more than sixty years ago, a lifestyle now vanished forever, and fast fading even from the memories of those who lived through those war and pre-war years. It seemed a good idea, too, to chronicle the beginnings of two Carmelite Monasteries in Yorkshire.

My readers may hear a chord they recognise, and find something they can appropriate for themselves and enjoy; for riches of the kind described here are multiplied mightily by being shared.

MTL
Wood Hall
October 1997

chapter one

Beginnings beside the Thames

One of my earliest memories is of looking up at the flowers of
sorrel in a hayfield. I must have been very small, probably three
years old, because the flowers were a lot taller than I, and seemed
to make a forest around me; but the tiny bright scarlet drops hung
down and trembled in the sunshine.

We moved from that area shortly afterwards, and it was a long
time before I met sorrel again and discovered its name. By then I
was much taller than the plant and saw it from above. Yet it had,
and still has, a mysterious beauty for me.

At each stage of my life the growing things around me have left
their own particular mark and fragrance on the event. At the time
I have often not been aware of it, yet looking back later the
memory has come of some plant or tree, or maybe a birdsong, that
was part of what happened, so that the sight of that particular plant
or the sound of that birdsong will automatically bring to mind the
essence of the event. This is probably everyone's experience, but
I had never noticed it until recently.

My parents lived in London after their marriage. They rented
a large room in which, to their joy, there was a piano. It was
perfectly adequate for their needs for the first two or three years,
but when the second baby was on the way they tried to get
somewhere with a little more space.

A friend, Lucy, who became a lifelong 'auntie' to the family,
suggested they took rooms in her parents' house in the village of
Horton near Windsor. It was a large old country house called
Home Close, and we rented two rooms: a large, pleasant living
room and a smaller bedroom leading from it. There was no tap or
sink or cooker of any kind. The house had a bathroom from which
Mother filled a jug of fresh water every day, and we managed with
that. A screen across one corner of the room kept the few cooking
utensils, washing-up, and pails of soaking baby-washing from being

9

too obtrusive. A small oil-stove, which sometimes smoked and blackened everything, was the only cooking facility. But Mother was young, and it was all part of the adventure of having a little home of her own. In those days (1931) this was quite a normal set-up, and she managed very well. She had never learnt to cook although – probably because – her mother had been an expert in the field. Many were the tales she used to tell in later years of the things they had to bury, or otherwise dispose of – particularly her first attempts at pastry and jam-making. The latter simply resisted all attempts to remove it from the jar and had to be thrown away in the end, jar and all.

Horton was a quiet village on the Thames, low-lying and often misty, but with some beautiful riverside walks. Milton had lived there for part of his life and wrote some of his loveliest works during that time. The house had a large garden and orchard. The old couple did not object to children enjoying themselves so by the time I was able to run about there was somewhere safe to play. When I was nearly two, my sister, Bou, was born. Her real name was Antoinette, but very early on she acquired the nickname Bou – pronounced Boo – and it has stayed with her to this day. Most of my recollections of those early years are of the two of us playing in the orchard, and on a swing made with a piece of rope that Mother had tied onto a branch for us, near the house. Sometimes she would sit and read to us on a mossy log, on sunny afternoons. I have liked mossy logs ever since!

There were nightingales there, which I am told sang in the tree just outside the windows; but I was too young to appreciate their song. Or perhaps I was asleep, and didn't hear it.

In the summer-time, when we were playing in the orchard we would sometimes hear the jingle of bells in the distance, growing gradually closer. We would race back to the house as fast as our legs could carry us, indoors and upstairs, shouting breathlessly, 'Ferrari! Ferrari!'. There would be a hasty consultation between my parents as they searched for a few coppers – there was always a lack of money in our house. We would try to get Father to come out with us, while we jumped up and down in sheer agony lest it would be too late and the jingling little cart would have passed by.

It seemed to take grown-ups so long to get down the stairs, along the driveway and onto the road. Oh, bliss, there it was – the little white horse-drawn ice-cream cart, with bells all along the sides of its canopy and Ferrari himself, a genial Italian, short, middle-aged, with a moustache, leaning over the side to see what we wanted. My parents always tried to buy something from anyone who came round the houses selling things. They knew from experience what it was to be hard up, and if they only had a few pence in the world they would still buy some little thing. Father loved Italians, and anything Italian, so he and Ferrari would have a chat, probably in Italian. We two children would stand by, admiring the horse and licking our ice-creams. Then off Ferrari would drive and the bells jingled and tinkled away into the distance.

Outings were rare, and in a sense unnecessary, as we had the run of a good part of the garden. When I look back, I think Mother must have found it rather confining. Mothers were very much tied to the home and the children in those days. Ordinary people did not have cars and money was so scarce. Once in a while, however, we did go out as a family to Windsor, which was fairly near. This was a great thrill – Windsor Castle, the guards outside it, the river with its pleasure boats, the shops and busy streets. All this appealed to Mother. While they lived in London, there had been plenty for her to see and do on foot; even after I was born, she could still get around with me in the pram and visit museums and places of interest. She loved the markets, even if she had nothing to spend; and there were always lots of people to watch. At Horton life must have been very quiet. However, we two little girls kept her quite busy and she was always a great reader. Though there was no piano in this flat, the elderly couple who owned the house had one in a rarely-used lounge and they let mother play it. She even had a couple of pupils, girls from the village.

She had taught piano and music theory before her marriage. She had left school at fourteen and begun work in a clothing factory. Music had been her great passion since she was a little girl; her family was very musical and she had had regular music lessons. One of her piano teachers had also given her singing

11

lessons, for she had a true and sweet voice. After leaving school she continued her music lessons and also went to night school, studying English and elocution. At seventeen, after passing the necessary exams, she became a music teacher, with a brass plate on the gate of their home – she was very proud of that. The photograph of this lovely young girl wearing her cap and gown always adorned the sitting-room of our home.

Apart from short gaps when there was no piano, she continued to teach music for an hour or so every day for the rest of her life. Even until she died, at the age of 80, she was still giving occasional lessons to her young grandchildren. She had a great gift with children – we used to say she could teach anyone to play. She knew just how to enter into their world and talk to them in their own language, and pass on to them some of her own enthusiasm and love for the piano. Sometimes her pupils were adults, but the vast majority were children. Often they were from families with very small incomes; but as she charged so little for her lessons they were able to benefit from her great musical gifts. She could have charged a lot more – it would have helped our own economic situation greatly – but neither she nor my father would have been happy to do so. It would have meant that only the better-off pupils could afford to learn. They loved to think of all those children – the 'have-nots', as they might be called today – being able to enter into the great world of music and enjoy making their own. Some of her pupils actually went on to make a career in music; but for most of them it was a new dimension to an otherwise fairly restricted life.

We stayed at Horton until I was six and Bou four, and by then another baby was on the way. Plans began to be talked over, photographs of houses looked at, and a lot of heart-searching done. We two children had already begun to put down roots, and entered with energy into the discussions, saying that if we went to live in another house there would *have* to be an orchard. We had grown to love playing among the trees and couldn't imagine life without them. Perhaps our demands did carry some weight.

Before leaving the area, my father took us to London, knowing that we were not likely to be going there again for a long time. It was one of his sudden ideas, but perhaps rather extravagant. Though she went along with it, I felt even at the time that Mother didn't really think it was a sensible thing to do, because money was so scarce. We went to Bertram Mills Circus, which at that time was very grand. We spent the night at an hotel, planning a visit to Madame Tussauds the following day. It was all very wonderful – and almost the best part was unpremeditated, for as we came out of the hotel in the morning, there on the pavement, surrounded by children, was a Punch and Judy show! We had never seen anything like it, and were thrilled, which gave an added joy to our parents. The whole outing and the visit to Madame Tussauds proved to be such a great success that we remembered and talked of it long afterwards. Even Mother liked to look back on the event despite her anxiety at the time. She was probably feeling the discomfort of pregnancy, too.

And so we left Horton, the occasional visits to Windsor and the walks by the pleasure-boats on the Thames; and we headed for Somerset.

chapter two

To the West Country

It was on a wintry January day that we saw the village of Ashcott for the first time. In years gone by, but at the time still remembered there, Ashcott had held its annual fair on that day, January 9th, and the local pubs had stayed open all day. By 1936 the two main fairs of the area were at Glastonbury, five miles away, and Bridgwater, some ten miles in the other direction. Bridgwater Fair was very old, and mentioned in the Domesday Book. The fairs still go on every year, and people from miles around buy and sell or just enjoy the fun there. Cattle and goods had been sold in the streets at Ashcott Fair too, and a local man, whom we knew well in later years, had played his fiddle on the village green while the young folk danced to his music.

We had travelled by train to Glastonbury. At that time, almost every small town and even village had its railway station. My father had gone in the removal van with our few pieces of furniture and Mother had the task of bringing the two little girls in the train – not easy, because we were a lively pair and the journey took several hours.

In years to come we were to get to know Glastonbury well; but at that time it seemed like a big, strange place. My father met us at the station, and took us to a small hotel where we were to spend our first night in Somerset. There was a lifesize cardboard figure of a monk pointing the way upstairs, which caught our imagination.

The next morning we all set off by bus for Ashcott, the village which was to become part of our lives, indeed part of ourselves for the rest of our lives. On that January morning, grey and cold, it must have looked rather bleak. But we children were excited at the thought of seeing our new home and prepared to be critical of it. If it didn't measure up to our hopes and expectations, there was going to be trouble. At six and four, we were able to give our views in no uncertain terms.

For our parents, all must have been quite different. This was their first home of their own, after having lived in rented rooms since their marriage. Though it was not yet paid for, it meant privacy, peace and freedom. Rooms had been satisfactory in that we had somewhere to live, with places for children to play both indoors and out. It was the large garden which we had found difficult to leave and which gave us a standard of comparison as we came to examine our new abode.

As we walked together up the road, which was only a small country lane then, we saw our house. Some two hundred years before, the wise builders had designed it so that the early morning sunshine shone cheeringly into the kitchen at the back of the house, where the housewife would spend much of the first part of the day, while the living room and bedrooms at the front had the benefit of its fuller warmth later on. Built of light grey Ham stone, with a red pantile roof, it stood close to the lane, with a garden at the side and the little orchard beyond. Many of the houses around had these little orchards, growing mainly cider apples, for this was cider country.

January daylight hours are short, so it was a blow to find that the electric lights, which we had expected to find in some of the rooms, were not working. Father set out to try to find someone who knew about electricity in the village. One of the neighbours kindly told him that he *thought* Mr Dibble knew something about mending fuses. Fortunately this man was at home and came along to look at the lights. He was able to make them work and we were deeply relieved to be able to see our way around the unfamiliar place, where boxes had been dumped haphazardly by the removals men. Mr Dibble told us that he too had a little daughter about our own age. It turned out that this little girl was to be our chief playmate for many years.

One of the first things we had to get accustomed to now that we were in Somerset was the local dialect. At first Mother found it very difficult to understand. If she asked the way around the village and was given detailed instructions, she was none the wiser, because she couldn't understand a word. In time we all adjusted and gradually began to pick up the intonation ourselves.

15

Most people who know anything about Somerset are familiar with the Mendips and the Quantocks, two long ranges of hills of great beauty which run for many miles and give the county its unique character. Not so many have heard of the Poldens, a lower, less dramatic, but still very lovely range that runs somewhere between the two, its ridge commanding magnificent views of both, with vast stretches of completely flat moors between. At that time they were always called the moors. I never heard them referred to as wetlands or levels, until quite recently. So I came to think of all moors as low-lying and flat, full of mystery, with their own flora and fauna, their rhines, peat, bulrushes and bog-grass. Although I must have known that Exmoor was high up, I didn't really connect it with a moor; so I was quite surprised when I came to live in Yorkshire and discovered that the Yorkshire moors, which I had always imagined were like the Somerset ones, were 'up'. The phrase 'up on the moors' rang strange to me for years. In fact, I think there's still a little place somewhere deep down in me that thinks *real* moors are 'down'.

The Poldens were our range. Ashcott was built on the steep side facing south-west, so that the village was sheltered from the north winds. We rarely had snow, even when it snowed on the Mendips and Quantocks. Perhaps they shielded us from it.

It was a self-contained village and many people rarely left it. At that time, only well-to-do people had a car, so there were few to be seen except those passing along the main Glastonbury–Bridgwater road. Although our house had electric lights in several of the rooms, there were no power points. Few people in the village would have had such things, or any appliances to run from them. It wasn't until after I had left home that the first point was put in the house – and it was a long time after that that the first electric fire, an ancient, second-hand one, was obtained.

There was mains water but the tap was just inside the garden wall from the road, so it was a good trek up and down from the house daily to bring it up to the kitchen in a white enamel jug. It all seems very primitive to us today, but it was perfectly normal then, and we felt we were lucky not to have to draw the water from a well. We knew the mains water was clean and fresh – though how often the jug was washed out is anybody's guess. But we all grew up strong and healthy on it, and it was lovely water to drink. We always knew that there was a deep well located somewhere beneath the stone-flagged courtyard, which had provided the water for previous generations. However, its exact position was not discovered for another forty years, when my younger brother excavated it, and found it to be a work of exquisite craftsmanship. There was also a well close to the house which collected the rainwater from the roof. The water was raised by a pump, and used for the garden generally; though as children we used to wash there sometimes because the water was so soft.

There was, of course, no flush toilet, or indeed any drains or pipes of any kind to get blocked or go wrong. A little outside lavatory, containing a seat over a large bucket, was the norm for nearly all the houses in the village. Because it involved going up the garden, whatever the weather, we tended not to use it except when we had visitors, when it was swept and polished. Chamber-pots in the house were simpler and my father was chief pail-emptier. Everything was dug back into the garden, providing humus and nutrients for future crops of vegetables and fruit, so nothing was wasted. I was amused recently when I heard of a cottage in an isolated position which was to be demolished as it was considered unfit for human habitation. The reason given was that it had no running water, electricity or sewage system! Using that standard of comparison, few of the houses in our village would have been deemed usable. No doubt, not so many years before that, even the palaces and houses of the great would have been similarly unequipped. It does make one realise how easily we become conditioned by our surroundings. Not many years before we went there, our house would have had no electricity and the well would have been in use, but generations were born and grew up happily there. Just a few times, when the lights failed for some reason, we used a large oil lamp, and it gave a gentle light well suited to those old, low-ceilinged rooms. Often we couldn't afford electric bulbs for upstairs rooms, and the hall and stairs had no lighting. We used small oil-lamps and candles frequently. Today these little lights would be looked upon as dangerous. They would

17

have been then, in careless hands; but growing up with them we learnt to take care.

There was very little furniture in the house at first, just the few things we had brought with us, a new bed and some chairs. Quite soon we obtained a large, round, polished table from a sale. My parents watched out for sales, where they bought things much more cheaply than anything available in shops. It was good furniture too, and would probably be very valuable by now. The big round table became very much a feature in our home and it is still owned by the family. A great joy for Mother was the day the piano came. She couldn't live very long without one. When it arrived, she felt that the house was really taking shape.

We two children looked at everything and took it all in. We settled ourselves into the new life, and explored our domain with satisfaction.

chapter three

A Somerset village in the 1930s

At that time, almost everything people needed for their everyday life could be bought in the village. The Post Office and Stores, situated at the side of the village green, could supply groceries, haberdashery, medicines, toys, and sometimes even clothes and shoes. Hob-nail boots for boys could also be bought there, and each spring strings of children's sandals were hung up outside, so mothers could set up their families in footwear for the summer. Although sweets, ice-creams and cakes were sold there, fresh cakes, buns and bread could be bought from one of the two bakers who came round the village with a van on different days of the week. We used to get brown loaves for my father, who liked brown best, from one of them, and white loaves, which were a little cheaper, for the rest of us from the other. Both baked all their own bread and cakes at their shop and the smell of the fresh baking as we went past was something wonderful – yet taken for granted. No one ever dreamed that bakers' shops would one day disappear, or at least become places without fragrance, with everything wrapped in plastic bags. Plastic wasn't known in Ashcott in 1936.

There was a butcher's shop too, and the butcher and his assistant came round the village twice a week, delivering orders and selling things such as sausages and faggots. Today's standards of hygiene did not apply then. Meat was cut up on a wooden slab with grubby hands, occasionally wiped on a rag, as was the sharp knife. No one was bothered, and unless memory has gilded the truth the meat and sausages were delicious.

Another trader who came round the village once a week was the fish-man. This character, whom we got to know quite well, came round on Friday mornings with a horse-drawn, covered cart. Refrigerators were rare then, and it was rumoured that he kept the fish behind the piano in his front room! Be that as it may, we usually bought some fish for Friday dinner because we were Catholics and meat was not allowed on that day. The fish-man also brought a little fruit in season. Mother would buy five bananas for sixpence. They were small and overripe but were considered a great treat. When the war came, he went into the Navy and his visits came to an end. We heard he had landed a congenial job looking after the Admiral's garden.

The High Street, apart from its situation towards the higher part of the hill, would have defeated Sherlock Holmes, had he been asked to spot it. It was just a lane, like any of the others, and we had been in the village some time before we discovered its name. Probably in past years it had been more important because at one end stood the church. This was very old and beautiful, not one of the spectacular churches for which Somerset is famed, but well worth exploring. In the days when Glastonbury Abbey was thriving, all these villages would have belonged to its area of care. Next to the church was an enclosed space with stone walls built like a little maze. This was the pound, where stray animals were put if they were found roaming around the lanes. They could be driven in, but could not find their way out until their owner collected them. I was quite sad when, years later, I heard that it had been demolished.

Also near the church was a derelict building which had once been the first school in Ashcott when education gradually became compulsory. In fact, many of the children were kept at home some of the time to help with the work, and none stayed there after they were twelve. The older inhabitants of the village had been to school there. We used to go in and look at the wooden benches, well carved with the penknives of generations of bored youngsters. About 1920 another school had been built, larger and better equipped, at the other end of the High Street. This one remained in use until the 1980s, when a more modern one, for primary children only, was built on another site.

There were two little shops in the High Street, both selling groceries and sweets, and sometimes fruit and vegetables in season. You could go to one for some items and the other for some cheese or butter and then down to the Post Office for the rest of your needs – and feel you had been shopping in a big way. One of these little shops also had a bookcase full of books which you could borrow for a penny per book for a week. This was the nearest thing to a library in the village, though the County Library delivered a crate of books regularly to the school, and one of the teachers there made an arrangement for us to borrow them.

The forge was also situated in that street. There were still horses around in good numbers, because all the local farmers used them for their work. The first tractors had not come to Ashcott as yet. The farms were small but comprehensive, each growing hay and grain with about a dozen milking cows, some with a few sheep, and most with pigs and poultry. Horses were all-important and much loved, and were shod at the forge. I still remember well the smell of the hot shoes being put on the horses' feet and wondering how these huge shires could be so patient as the blacksmith nailed them on.

Halfway along the High Street was the Ring o' Bells, aptly named for its nearness to the church, which had a good peal. Ashcott was well off for public houses; the Ashcott Inn was on the main road, and there was the Albion at the far end of the village. At the other end stood the Pipers Inn, where Judge Jeffreys, of ill-repute in Cromwell's time, was said to have stayed; this was more of an hotel, despite its name. Besides all these, several of the local farms had their own cider-presses and made many gallons of the heady brew for themselves. These presses must have been little changed over the centuries. They were made of two wooden boards with a wooden trough to catch the apple juice as the fruit, mixed with straw, was crushed gradually by a turn of the screw-handle. Apples in the orchards were left to drop from the trees and raked into long piles called graves. We used to think that half of them must be rotten and certainly as we approached the orchards we could smell cider. A day would come, however, when the farmer would come along and shovel them all into his cart. Then into the cider press they went. 'But what about all the slugs, Daddy?' we would ask. Evidently they became part of the brew. There was nothing else added to that cider – no yeast or any other agent. It was just the apple juice which fermented by itself and made a powerful drink. The layers of straw in the press were to facilitate the drainage of the juice into the trough. The compressed apple pulp and straw was called 'cheese' and was used afterwards as cattle-feed. I wonder if anyone makes cider like that today?

When we first lived in Ashcott, it was still the custom to toll the church bell when anyone died. This was an ancient Christian custom, alerting the villagers to pray for the soul of the dead person. It also meant that everyone knew there had been a death in the village. Heads would peep out of doorways and windows to see if anyone knew who it was, before deciding who it was most likely to be. Word soon got round of the true identity of the deceased, although no-one had a phone except the policeman and the Post Office. The bell was tolled again on the day of the funeral.

The presence of the village policeman was an important factor in the life of the village. His house was almost opposite ours. Every day we would see him setting out on his beat, wearing his cloak and helmet, and riding his bike. He would patrol the village and its surrounding roads. A big, strong man, he was much respected by the locals, at least by the more law-abiding among them. He once told my father that his motto was "live and let live". I'm not sure how far he applied this in general when he met with breaches of the law. Nowadays the nearest policeman is three miles away at Street, or maybe even further away, and the villagers no longer feel so safe. In the 1930s little children – and bigger ones – could walk for miles or play safely anywhere without their parents having to be anxious about them. It was a world of greater freedom.

The roads, called lanes by most people, were swept and the verges trimmed by a little team of men paid by the local council. They worked their way around the village at a leisurely pace with a wheelbarrow, spades and brooms, tidying up as they went along. Somehow they managed to appear at the best vantage point when anything was going on in the village – near the church when there was a wedding or funeral, near the pubs when some function was on, etc. They didn't miss much, but it was a poorly-paid job, and looked on as being rather a come-down by most people. Even farm hands were a degree further up the scale in general estimation. Yet, when I look back, how hard their lives must have been! The farm labourers worked from morning until night every day, even part of Sunday because the milking and feeding of the animals had to go on, yet their wages were only ten shillings and sixpence a week. This had to pay the rent of their cottages and keep themselves, their wives and their children. If they were ill or off work for some reason, then there was no pay for that day. Even if they were not able to work because of bad weather conditions, it was still 'no work – no pay'. There was no question of a holiday or even going anywhere. Many of the children were often ragged and dirty and had lice in their hair; they must have been cold in the winter. Even tiny tots played on the roads, and every year impetigo and all the other contagious diseases swept through the village. There were no antibiotics; I remember a little boy of six dying of measles. The mothers had a tough time; there were none of the labour-saving gadgets that we are so accustomed to today. Many had no mains water; none of us had hot water on tap. One got hot water by boiling it in a kettle. Washing-up liquids and detergents were unheard of. However, what we now think of as deprivation was by no means seen as such at the time – no doubt future generations will think of these present days as deprived. There were lots of pleasures, many of which are gone now, to be replaced by television and holidays abroad. Everyone was in the same boat, so to speak, and it was a good boat to be in, and a steady one.

When I visited the village fifty years later and saw the young mothers popping the toddlers into their car-seats and driving off to town to do the shopping, I realised what a vast change had taken place. The little ones looked so healthy and warmly-dressed. I could see that, in some ways at least, it was a change for the better.

Our parents on their graduation days

chapter four

A village economy

There is so much more I remember about Ashcott in those early days. As most of it will soon have gone from living memory, I thought it worth jotting down a few more things.

In the 1930s there were several other small businesses that served the community and rendered it unnecessary for people to go out of the village. There was Mr Isgrove, the saddler, who made all the leather equipment for the farm horses. Wearing an apron, he sat stitching the leather in his shop. Not far away from him Mr Farrow, the local joiner and carpenter, had his workshop. This was a long open barn where he made many things, including all the coffins, for he was also the undertaker. All the sawing was done by hand in those days, of course. He was a fine craftsman, and in the evenings pursued his hobby of making carved coffee tables. He also played the organ at the church.

Further up the hill, Mr Baker had his barber's shop. He cut men's and boys' hair, and sold a few things like Woodbine cigarettes and matches. He was a very kind man, and good with small children who didn't like having their hair cut.

Milk was delivered to the door, as it is today, but in less sterile conditions – Mr Everdell came round with his horse and trap, a couple of milk churns, a pail, and a dipper. He filled the pail from one of the churns, brought it to the door, and measured out the required amount with the dipper into the customer's jug. The churns were tall, heavy metal cans which must have held about ten gallons apiece. All farmers put their milk straight into these after milking; they were then put outside on a stand beside the farm gate for collection in the early mornings by Wilts United Dairies' milk lorry, unless the farmer had his own milk round.

Another amenity was the Bridgwater Steam Laundry. A man came round in a motor-van once a week, and collected the parcels of washing. It was certainly a great help if you could get sheets washed there. Most of the housewives in the village had a copper and could boil their white laundry, when they had the firewood to heat it. Mother only had a bowl on the kitchen table, and a domestic-size kettle on the oil-stove. She washed woollies beautifully, and most of the other things, but she found sheets and my father's shirts almost impossible to launder as they were made of cotton or linen. (Drip-dry or non-iron fabrics had not yet been invented.) So, now and again, these were sent to the laundry. I say 'now and again' because each article cost a penny or more to be washed, so it all had to be well thought out, and resulted in our using sheets until they were decidedly grey. The laundry van ceased coming round when the war began, so from then on Mother had to manage as well as she could.

Charlie Bobbet could sole and heel shoes, in a fairly rough and ready but serviceable way; and 'Uncle' Hancock soldered pots and pans. These two delightful characters shared a little cottage adjoining the Reading Room, and grew vegetables in the garden there. The Reading Room was no longer in use for its original purpose by the time we came to live in Ashcott, but it was sometimes used for small functions. It was probably built in Victorian times by one of the local benefactors of the village. Another amenity that was rarely used by then and was soon to become obsolete was a water-trough for horses. This had a tap and an iron cup chained to it for the use of thirsty humans and underneath a smaller drinking-trough for dogs, cats and other small creatures. Above, carved in the stone wall, were Coleridge's words:

He prayeth well who loveth well
Both man and bird and beast.

This refreshment was situated exactly opposite the Ashcott Inn. Maybe the donor hoped that by providing a free drink of water he was lessening the likelihood of the villagers spending their money in the pub. In time the tap ceased to function, and the trough dried up; when I revisited the village many years later the whole thing had gone. We knew it so well; it was where we waited for the bus that ran regularly between Bridgwater and Glastonbury.

Although few people had a car, the transport services were

26

good. There were buses regularly throughout the day and early evening; we could also catch a bus to Taunton if we walked down as far as the Pipers Inn. But Taunton was about seventeen miles away and few of the villagers felt the need to venture that far. As well as the main-route buses, there was the one belonging to Mr Dibble. He ran his own bus service between Ashcott and Bridgwater, not along the usual route but through the lower-lying villages at the edge of the moor which had no public transport. He went to and fro several times a day, with an extra trip on market day, whatever the weather. He would pick up parcels for people and drop them off at the appropriate place, and generally provided a much-needed service until he retired.

There was also Ashcott station. Admittedly, it was a two-and-a-half mile walk across the moor, but trains ran regularly between Burnham, Highbridge and Glastonbury. These lines connected with the Great Western Railway, and on the few occasions that he needed to do so my father was able to be in London by 11 a.m., providing that he had made an early start by cycling to the station. It was a tiny station – just a single track with its little platform, station-master's house, level-crossing gates and signal box. We thought it very exciting, although it was rare indeed that we used it. We went as far as we could walk and that was the extent of our roaming. Until much later, none of us had bicycles except my father – and to Mother's relief he didn't have his for long. The result was that we knew the area in which we lived very well indeed; the nearby towns on the bus route fairly well as we grew older; but never had the opportunity of exploring much beyond this, except through reading.

Medically, the village was well served. Two doctors from Street and Glastonbury each ran a surgery in a private house two days a week. But doctors had to be paid and were only called on in great need. The main source of help, healing and comfort for all and sundry was that unforgettable woman, the District Nurse. She lived right at the centre of the village beside the village green – or what was left of it. It was called The Batch, and the huge tree that stood in the middle was reputed to mark the central spot of Somerset. In our early days she rode a bicycle, but quite soon, to everyone's delight and approval, she acquired a little car which stood on the Batch when not in use. Nurse was available whenever she was wanted, day or night, rain or shine. Everyone began to feel better the moment she greeted them with her kindly smile. She was called out to all the births and all the dyings, to helpless old men, to little children with measles. Nothing was too much trouble. In theory, she had a day off each week, when she put on ordinary clothes instead of her familiar navy uniform. Everyone did their best to observe this day, which they felt she should have, yet if there was a sudden emergency no-one feared to go along and knock on her door. Hers was truly a vocation. She loved all her patients, rejoiced with them in their return to health, and helped them in their anxieties. She saw the younger members of our family into the world, assisting the doctor from Street, and found time to enter into the play of the older children on her way in or out of the home. Everyone loved Nurse.

All this helped to give a sense of stability to the village. Whatever kind of help was needed, it was never far away. Though people didn't have telephones of their own, there was always a neighbour or someone who would run with a message to Nurse, the policeman, the grocer, or whoever was needed. There was a public telephone outside the Post Office from which one could ring up a doctor or ambulance in real need. Ordinary medicines and ointments, aspirins, wintergreen, syrup of figs, sticking-plaster and the like could be bought at the Post Office shop.

Although this same shop also had what was called the drapery department, where you could buy wool, needles and cottons, patterns, and sometimes even children's and ladies' dresses, there was no shop that actually sold fabrics. To remedy this, a man came round once a month from a shop in Langport with samples of all kinds of material. Customers chose what they wished and ordered the required amount, and he would bring it the next time he called. Mother used to make our little summer frocks, and there would be great excitement when this man arrived in the spring and we could choose the material for them from his pattern-book. The choice was very limited by today's standards, but to us it was an important matter – even more so to Mother who had to keep a strict eye on the price. The prettiest ones were always too expensive at seven or eightpence a yard. 'Look at this lovely one with little blue flowers on!' she would say encouragingly. 'And it's only six-three a yard'. This meant 6¾ d, because farthings were still in use. Some were even 5½d a yard. There were 240 pence in a pound and a penny was quite a lot of money – in fact, riches to a child.

Then there was the oil-man. He came round all the villages once a week. From him we bought the paraffin for the oil-stove and lamps. But he didn't only have paraffin on board. His was a remarkable vehicle, a kind of lorry with open sides lined with deep shelves. The paraffin was in a tank slung below and he filled our drum from this. On the shelves, and hanging on hooks, and piled on top, were innumerable things for sale: cups, plates, kettles, brooms, dusters, doormats, fire-lighters, matches, soap, – all kinds of household wares. He always had some bargain that he felt we really ought to buy. When the war came he even had toys on board, which people had made and asked him to sell for them.

When I revisited Ashcott in 1988, there was still an oil-man coming round – not the same man but it could well have been the same lorry. By that time he also sold washing-up liquid, paper hankies, toilet paper, fly-sprays and other amenities unheard of in our childhood days, but by now necessities of life. My family thought he only came for Mother's sake; and for an old lady unable to walk very far, it made her life a lot easier. She even bought quite a few of her Christmas presents from him – things like torches, pretty cups and saucers, and coloured trays.

These regular tradesmen were all very useful, and meant there was little need to go outside the village for shopping. Apart from these fixtures built into the rhythm of the months, there were also itinerant salesmen who knocked on the door hoping to sell their wares. I remember a gentle Indian wearing a turban, but otherwise european clothes, with a large suitcase full of small things such as shoe-laces, cottons, needles, press-fasteners, hooks and eyes and tape measures. Even if at the time we were not in need of any of these, and had hardly any cash in the house, my parents always tried to buy something. They were very sensitive to anyone in need and, as is so often the case, would help however little they had themselves. The same applied when the gipsies came round selling their clothes pegs, and begging for old clothes.

On rarer occasions, the knife-grinder came. He rode a tricycle and would come to the door to see if we had any scissors, knives or shears to sharpen. He was very poor and ragged, and stood in the lane beside his tricycle sharpening away -- not always very satisfactorily. Once he brought his wife with him and said she mended door mats. I rather think ours was beyond redemption at the time so we declined that offer. When Mother heard that his wife was with him, she gave Bou and me a cup of tea to take out to her. It was a cold day and we found she had a baby in a tattered old pram; she poured the tea into the baby's bottle and fed it. I have always remembered this poignant incident.

chapter five

"A son, Sir!"

This was the village which was to be the framework for our lives, the place where those all-important growing and rooting stages were to be accomplished - or at any rate given a good start. We two little girls, with our flaxen pigtails and brown eyes, found a stable world there. We didn't realise it at the time, and took everything for granted. With eagerness and wonder we explored our immediate surroundings, getting to know the names of the plants and wild flowers in the confines of our own garden and small orchard. To begin with we didn't go further afield on our own; but we didn't need to do so, for there was endless scope for play and make-believe so close at hand. We played all day long, mostly out of doors or in the old farm-buildings, only coming in for meals and sleep.

Then some official came round to see why it was that we were not attending school. Bou was just five by then and I was nearly seven. So for a while we went to the village school and though this did not last long I was grateful for our time there. The most far-reaching result was that in a comparatively short time we got to know the people in the village. Anyone moving into the village – a rare occurrence then – was a 'foreigner' and continued to be looked upon as one for many years. Even people from towns not far away were 'foreign', so a family like ours, coming from the London area and with no previous connection with the village, was viewed with considerable suspicion. Even by the time the war came, there were those who thought my father might be a spy. If we had not had that time among the children of the village I think we would never have been accepted as we were, and certainly it would have taken our parents a long time to get to know the inhabitants. Children learn so rapidly at that age, and very soon if Mother or Father asked us, 'Who's that lady in the red coat?' we could inform them that it was Pamela's mum, and she lived at the top of school hill – and we even had lots more information to give about her family. So this time was one of integration for us all into the social fabric of the village.

Whilst on the subject of school, I feel I must pay tribute to the teachers who spent all their lives teaching at that small rural school. For more than forty years they were amongst the most important and respected people in the area. Everyone had been through their hands, either as pupil or young parent, or both. Miss Tilke, who taught the infants class, became a close friend of our family and came to be called 'auntie'. She had lived in the village all her life, teaching, and caring for her mother. As well as the Infants Class, which was comprised of four, five and six-year-olds up to and including what was known as Standard One, she taught the girls from all three classes needlework, knitting, weaving and other crafts. She also played the piano for the daily hymn at assembly and was in the playground at break when we all ran wild for a few minutes. A tall lady with silvery strands in her hair, which was worn in a bun, she must have been still quite young when we were there, but we thought of her as middle-aged. Certainly she had wonderful energy and used all her time and gifts to help the children. She had a kindly face and chuckle and it was quite obvious that she really loved all her charges – though she knew how to correct rascals; never cross or out of sorts, she always listened to both sides before administering justice. We felt that she knew we were trying, even though the result wasn't very good, and left much to be desired. By the time we reached Standard One, pencils were abandoned in favour of pens and ink, and we wrote in proper exercise books. I still recall the huge blots on my writing book and how powerless I felt to stop them coming – I suppose I dipped my pen too far into the ink so it had no option but to make blots; but I didn't understand that at the time. Children today are spared the misery of those pens and ink-wells

Miss Tilke was also in charge of the County Library books, which were delivered regularly to the school. She was a great reader, and encouraged both the children and their parents to read. Those library books were a life-line for our own mother, who had been accustomed to having a library within reach. Books could be ordered in advance, and there was a good selection in each consignment. Miss Tilke always referred to them as the 'liberry books' and this became a household pronunciation with us.

Even in the school holidays Miss Tilke didn't go away – she was so keen to do everything for her charges. She would cut out patterns for their needlework, prepare classes, and study Child Education books to glean ideas for communicating skills to little ones. There must have been hundreds of people who owed their early training to Miss Tilke.

The other two teachers in the school were Mr and Mrs King. Mr King taught the top class, which consisted of the twelve and thirteen-year-olds. He also taught all the boys woodwork and gardening while the girls were doing their needlework and handicrafts. It was he who was called on to dispense justice when arbitration had failed. His was the last word and he alone administered the strap. This leather strap hung on the wall of his classroom and was not often used, only for great or persistent crimes. The boy (I don't think it was ever a girl) had to hold out his hand and receive two or three smart smacks with the strap. It was not so much the pain, though it must have hurt a bit, but the opinion of the rest of the class that made it a dreaded punishment. Everyone witnessed it and knew that the recipient must have really earned it. Mr King was a kindly man and rarely made use of punishment – it was not his way. However, the threat of the strap helped him out of a few difficult situations.

Mrs King taught the middle class. Hers was probably the most difficult task, because some of her children were only just seven; some were working for their Eleven Plus exam, and the others had to fit in between. She was an excellent teacher, however, and coped well, even putting on quite advanced plays for the Christmas end-of-term celebration.

Over the years I have often looked back and been amazed at the amount Mrs King and Miss Tilke taught me. All children soak up knowledge rapidly in their early years, but I'm sure their teaching methods must have been very good for so much to have gone into our heads and stayed there. Miss Tilke taught me all the basics of needlework, including how to do French seams, run-and-fell, and various embroidery stitches. It was Mrs King who first introduced me to the wonderful stories in the Bible, such as David and Goliath, Elijah being fed by the ravens, and Elijah's servant seeing the little cloud as big as a man's hand. This gave me the interest to read them for myself and explore the Bible further – a passion that has never really left me.

We made friends with the children, though they regarded us cautiously and wanted to know why we didn't 'talk proper'. They taught us a lot; probably children teach other children as much as the teachers do.

Quite soon, however, my parents obtained permission to teach us at home, for which they were well qualified; and so began the 'Litchfield School' as we liked to call it. It was wonderful – we had occasional lessons, perhaps a whole morning of algebra – but did lots of reading on our own and had plenty of play. About this time a man came to the door taking orders for a new encyclopaedia designed for older children. It was called *The Book of Knowledge,* eight large well-printed tomes edited by Harold F B Wheeler. It was beautifully bound and was, of course, very expensive. To Mother's initial horror, my father ordered a set. It must indeed have seemed a crazy thing to do, since we could often afford only the bare necessities of life; but it proved to be a stroke of genius. Mother herself soon realised that it was one of the best things they ever bought. How we loved those books! They were an education in themselves, and as the years went by we absorbed more and more of their contents. They also let both of our parents off the hook on many occasions – when faced with a battery of unanswerable questions, they could say, 'See if it's in the *Knowledge Books*', and that would send us hurrying off to look it up in the appropriate volume.

Father taught us mathematics, Latin and French – or tried to, I should say. Mother's lessons were the more practical ones; needlework and hand-work of various kinds; cookery, and, of course, music. I realise now that we must have been very trying, for she longed for us to play well and enjoy it. I did enjoy it secretly, but there is something about being told – or even asked – to practise that instantly puts some children off. I'm afraid that we were a bit uncooperative. It was Mother who guided all our reading, too, and she was brilliant at this. She knew exactly what books we were nearly ready for and kept us just a bit ahead of our capacity, so that reading became for us a continuing joy and a big part of our lives.

One July day in that first summer at Ashcott, Bou and I ran up the orchard in the morning to carry on with our latest project. We were digging a deep hole under an apple tree using little pieces of broken iron rain-pipe as tools, and were going to make a dam. I cannot think now where we thought the water would come from, but it was very real to us at the time. It was a glorious, hot summer's day and we stayed out digging and digging, chattering away non-stop to each other as we always did. When it was nearly dinner-time, to our delight Father came striding up the slope of the orchard towards us. He was carrying a frying-pan with some sausages in, still sizzling and smelling very good. 'Mum isn't very well so I thought I'd bring some dinner out for you', he said. We thought what a brick he was – now there was no need to go indoors.

So we stayed out all the day until about six in the evening. Then he called us in, and took us to the foot of the stairs. 'Listen!' he said. There was a strange wailing sound coming from the far bedroom. One of us said, 'it's the cat!'

'It's your baby brother!' he corrected, and he took us upstairs to peer into the cot for our first glimpse of Simon. In those days children were told nothing about forthcoming births, so it was a great surprise and we were very excited. We only learnt in later years that Father had had a hectic day getting the things the doctor and nurse needed for the birth, and trying to make sure that we didn't come in and get in the way. No doubt he was also feeling very anxious, for it was Mother's first confinement at home, and he worried lest something should go wrong. He hadn't had a moment all day to shave, but at half-past five had just lathered up his chin when there was a tap on the kitchen door. As he stood in front of the mirror, brush in hand, the District Nurse put her head in. 'A son, sir', she announced happily, 'Ten minutes ago'. Picking up a pencil, he wrote on the wall, '5.20 p.m. July 11th' and that information stayed there for many a year.

As time went on, we found having a baby brother could be a mixed blessing. We were very proud of him and loved him dearly; but it seemed such a long time to wait before he could really join in our games. I had always wanted a brother, like the ones in stories, but they were usually older and could do things, make things, and help people escape from danger. This one required minding when we would rather have run off to play on our own.

Meanwhile Father endeavoured to cultivate the garden and grow as much as possible in the way of vegetables and fruit. There were already apple trees in the orchard and sixty gooseberry bushes in the garden, where they did double-duty as hedges. There were plum and pear trees, loganberries trained over the wall, and some wild raspberries, all well established by the previous owners. Father hoped to grow vegetables for our own consumption and for sale, and thereby supplement his income. He loved gardens, and though he hadn't done a lot before coming to Somerset, he asked advice and gleaned all the information he could. What he hadn't bargained for, and what ultimately defeated him, was the very difficult soil condition of that garden. It was heavy clay over limestone and was either too sodden and heavy to dig or solid as a rock. For a strong man it would have been more possible – indeed, he did absolute marvels considering the difficulty. He had lost the use of his right arm in World War One, yet managed to do nearly everything. In those days there weren't the helps for disabled people that are available now. It was remarkable the amount he produced. We always had plenty of vegetables and salad for ourselves, but there was rarely enough to sell – and my parents weren't very business-like about selling. They much preferred to give things away. The only produce we ever made any money on was the gooseberries, which we children used to help pick and deliver to people's houses. We knocked on their doors and proudly handed in the well-filled bag or basket. The housewives had ordered the amount they required beforehand and we collected the money: twopence a pound until the war came, and then threepence. Of course, this was before decimal currency, so we were selling 120 pounds of gooseberries for £1. But it is

36

nonsensical to make a comparison because the value of money is now totally different.

Father persevered with the garden for a good many years, in fact until we had grown up on his good vegetables and left home. We all regret that we didn't help him more. We did help in spurts, a lot as we grew bigger, but it did not have the same attraction as playing, so we were often rather grudging in our response to his suggestion. I don't think we realised until long after we had grown up how immensely difficult it must have been to use a spade, fork, or any other tool, with only one hand, and the left one at that. Wheel-barrows were an impossibility, as were shears. We simply took it for granted that he could do things, and never thought to offer help, not even with the mowing of the front lawns, which he did with a small push mower. There were no power tools in those days, even for professionals, but because such things had never even been thought of there was no hardship in this. After all, the land had been farmed, houses built, and even all the great cathedrals erected over the centuries, entirely with hand tools, and many were the skilled craftsmen who used them.

An early photo of Marie

Bou and Marie, aged 4 and 6

chapter six

Sorrow and joy

One summer evening, after we two girls had gone to bed and Simon was safely tucked up in his cot, Bou and I heard Mother playing the piano downstairs. This was not unusual; often the hour after we'd gone upstairs was her first opportunity of playing in the day, and she loved to sit at the piano after a busy day of cooking, washing and other motherly tasks. Yet that evening was different. The air was warm and full of the scents of the summer garden and the window of the front room, where the piano was, was open. The little casement of our bedroom was also pegged open and together we listened enthralled to what seemed to us to be the most wonderful music we had ever heard. We crept out of our room and gradually down the stairs, a step at a time, to get closer to the source of this delight. When the piece ended, we sat there on the bottom step for a few moments. It was absolutely forbidden to come downstairs once we'd gone to bed, but on that occasion we pushed open the door of the room where Mother was and went in. 'What was it?' we asked, still quite enraptured. At first she was not at all pleased at our appearance but, when she realised why we had come, she told us that it was Beethoven's *Moonlight Sonata* – and that we must go back to bed AT ONCE.

The next morning we were still full of the thought of the music, and wanted to know who Beethoven was. Mother was busy cooking the dinner and took the easy way out by referring us to the *Books of Knowledge*. Soon we were back again. 'He's not even mentioned', I said miserably. 'He must be. He's one of the most famous composers', she replied. 'Go and have another look'. Back we went, looking at Bai, Bate, Bay . . . no luck. Then Mother must have tumbled to our dilemma and came in. 'It's spelt Beethoven. He's German', she said.

So from then on, we were hooked. We read all we could find about Beethoven in those books and various others, and this led on to our finding out about the other great masters of music – Mozart, Haydn, Handel, Chopin and several others. We entered a new world, where all these people became our friends. We were lucky in that we had a great many books. One whole wall of the living-room was a built-in bookcase, which was one of the first things Father had had put up when the joiner had come to mend the holes in the floor in our early days. That room had a wooden floor but most of the others had stone flags. Both of our parents would have been far more likely to spend their last penny on a second-hand book than on a cup of tea or bun.

We were, of course, merely children, and our love for these great people was bounded by the limitations of childhood. All the same, a new door had been opened to us that would never again close, but rather would admit us further and further into a very wonderful world. We wanted to hear their music played, and even felt inspired to try to play some of the simpler pieces ourselves. 'It's Schumann's birthday today!' I bounced into the kitchen to announce one day – and I still remember the date now.

Both Mother, and in a much smaller measure I myself, used to play some of these lovely tunes while Simon was in his pram near the piano; Mother had the idea that it helped him to get off to sleep for his mid-day nap. In fact, he must not only have been listening intently but actually taking in that music far more deeply than we ever dreamt a baby or toddler could. To this day he has an extraordinary depth of musical appreciation. He doesn't just know all the music but all the *notes* of the music; and he loves it passionately.

Bou and I had a kind of shared yet private hobby which we called our 'thinks'. We each had a story going on in our heads, which had new instalments added daily during quiet times, mainly when we went to bed, before sleep overtook our minds. Sometimes we would tell each other what was happening in our 'thinks'. Once we had discovered the composers, they all found their places in the story, and became known by their Christian names – Amadeus, Ludwig, and so on. They were very real.

Another character from bygone days whom we held in high esteem was Robin Hood. The only time we ever ran away from home was when we felt compelled to go and live as outlaws in a stretch of woodland known as Fifteen Acres, 'The Secret Wood' to us. We had seen a play which a company from Bridgwater had put on in the Village Hall and which had fired our imagination. We had no idea what an outlaw was but, because Robin Hood was one we felt it would be a good thing to imitate him. We set off after dinner one sunny summer afternoon, armed with home-made bows and arrows and quarter-staves. These last were simply strong sticks, but in the tip we used to fix – most hazardously – a sliver of broken glass that ended in a sharp point. How we didn't cut ourselves inserting these I can't imagine, but we were quite accustomed to playing with these weapons. Thus armed, we felt well protected from any attack.

We reached the wood, quite a long walk from our home, and seeming longer than usual because we had never been there on our own before. It was always Father who took us for long walks and who explored with us the surrounding countryside. The first thing we decided to do was to select a place for a camp. We prowled around for a bit but somehow our consciences were beginning to make us feel ever so slightly uncomfortable. Also we were getting hungry, for it hadn't occurred to us to bring anything with us to eat and it was past our teatime. So one of us had the bright idea that *this* visit to the wood could simply be an exploratory one, and that we would return at a later date with the equipment we might need. So home we went, as quickly as we could, to find our parents frantic. We had never gone away from the garden before and they had called and searched to no avail. They were very cross – partly in sheer relief to see that we were unharmed. In fact, we hadn't thought of how they would feel at all, only of the lovely adventure of going off to be outlaws. Needless to say, we never tried again. I think this episode happened when we were still quite small, before we met the composers.

One of the great gifts that Mother gave us was her love of poetry. I did not realise until comparatively recently that poetry is a language, and, like any other language, has to be learned. People do learn it at any age, at least to a certain extent – and indeed it is never too late to begin. But the very best time of all is when one is very young. In the same way as a child who hears two languages daily grows up to be bi-lingual, so one who hears poetry read long before she can read it for herself, grows into an understanding of that language. She will not always understand the poetry, for some poems give up their full content very slowly, only over years of reading, and some actually seem inexhaustible in depth. But there is a way of being at home in the presence of poetry, able to follow its music with ease, just as one who had always been able to speak a foreign language will recognise and interpret it immediately she hears it. Mother read poetry to us often, and because it meant so much to her she read it beautifully.

I always thought I had never heard anyone read poems so well as she did, but over the years I began to wonder if perhaps my memory was coloured by nostalgia and affection. However, I had the great privilege of going to help her briefly when she was a very old lady, frail and unwell. I took her for a tiny jaunt to the nearby town of Street by taxi, and she was able to walk with difficulty into one or two shops. She had always loved shopping, or at any rate seeing what was for sale, and she was delighted to go into a bookshop and choose a book. This was a new selection of modern poetry. When we got home, I settled her in her chair and went to prepare tea. When I came back with the tray, there she was, deep in the book, peering at its pages with her failing sight. "Listen to this", she exclaimed, her voice full of the thrill of another beautiful new experience. And as she read to me I knew my memory had not played me false. Later that evening, I read a couple of the poems to her, and despite my poor rendering her enjoyment and satisfaction brought to my own eyes a new vision of life

The Christmas when I was eight, an apparently very small incident occurred which was to have a profound effect on the whole of my life, and indeed that of all of our closely-knit family. Auntie Lucy gave me for Christmas a life of St Thérèse of Lisieux, written for children. We were already great readers, so there was nothing unusual about having a book given to us; it was always a very welcome gift – except when someone gave us a book intended for younger children, and which we felt it beneath our dignity to be seen reading.

St Thérèse was not, of course, in that category. I read it over and over again, and decided that I, too, would be a Carmelite one day. But children change, and over the years I had lots of other dreams of what I should become when I grew up. In turn, I was going to be a dancer, a musician, a poet, a writer, and for some time I was going to fly. I learned all I could about flying and air navigation at one stage. On and off I was always going to be a writer; and just now and again the idea of being a nun would peep back for a bit. I have to admit I find it puzzling when I ask my nieces and nephews and other children what they'd like to be when they grow up and invariably receive the reply that they don't know. At the time of my own childhood, children were usually aiming at being something specific, even though this often changed as they grew older. Perhaps it is because there are so many options open nowadays. Or maybe they are realistic enough to know that the future is not so firmly in their own hands. They have grown up with the shadow of unemployment hovering close. Perhaps we were a bit starry-eyed, to believe that we could do anything we wanted and that everything was within our reach, given desire and perseverance!

What we were unaware of in those years of the late 1930s was our parents' anxiety over the growing political tension throughout Europe. We heard them talking about the prime minister, the heads of state, the Nazi regime, but it all sounded very dull and we paid little heed. Gradually a more ominous note crept into their discussions, and when people came to see them they endlessly seemed to talk politics.

Then, on 3rd September 1939, came that inevitable day which everyone had dreaded, when war began. There had been high winds the previous night and a few tiles had blown off our roof. Two young brothers who lived down the road came with a ladder and fixed them back on for us. Afterwards they came inside and sat in the living-room to listen with us to the announcement on the wireless (as it was called then) as they did not have one. I can still remember the announcer's voice as he gave the solemn and heartbreaking information: 'ENGLAND IS AT WAR WITH GERMANY'.

What Father's thoughts were at that moment we never could have fathomed. It was less than twenty years since he had come out of hospital after prolonged surgical attempts to save his ruined arm, after surviving Passchendaele. The 'war to end all wars', at the cost of so much blood, had won so short a time of peace. Typically, however, Father wrote to the War Office offering his services: could he be of any help, perhaps as an interpreter? The fact that he was nearing fifty and had only one arm did not seem an impediment to him. Mercifully for us all his offer was not accepted, though neither was it turned down: it would be 'borne in mind'. For a good while afterwards he worked hard at bringing his Italian up-to-date, shutting himself away with his books, or sitting listening to the news in Italian on the wireless. Later on in the war, when Italian prisoners were sent to work on various local farms, he would seek them out and have long chats with them in their own language. It must have been a comfort to them because few, if any, of the people around spoke any Italian.

I have many memories of the war. It was the background to those formative years of our lives, against which we see ourselves as we look back. I say we, but mainly it was Bou and I, because Simon was only just three when war was declared, not old enough to register its enormity as clearly as we were. There was much that we ourselves were too young to understand, or even notice.

The immediate anguish for our parents was the fact that Mother was eight months pregnant. The thought of bringing a new, innocent little life into the chaotic world of war was a very frightening one. Yet they coped, as the people around us coped, carrying on with their day-to-day living as well as they could and doing their best to help those around them do the same.

On October 9th, our new sister, Bridget, was born. She was beautiful, with large, dark-brown eyes that surveyed her new surroundings with interest, as though she were thinking deeply. Mother had her at home, in the bedroom furthest from the stairs, which was quiet. Simon had been born there, and we later discovered that people who had lived in that house many years before had all chosen that room for their confinements. In years to come Julian, too, first saw the light of day there.

I was detailed to help with the washing and cooking, and felt immensely proud of my new responsibilities. Bou had to look after Simon, who at the age of three was at the stage when he needed continual attention. She really had a very difficult task, and one that didn't have such outward show as mine had. I was given a white apron – someone must have sent it to us – which I wore to show how important and efficient I was! I didn't realise how hard this must have been for Bou; but she took it all with her customary largeness of heart. Mother had recently taught me how to make pastry. She felt, I believe, that if Father had his apple pies now and again all would be well. I used to play with the ball of pastry – poor, wartime pastry, but just as much fun to play with! – throwing it up to the blackened ceiling, and making shapes with it. Ultimately, I rolled it out, by now decidedly grey in colour, and put it on my pie-dish of apples. Father, bless him, used to say how delicious it was and never had he tasted such pastry. This was quite possibly true! But from then I was convinced that I was a good cook.

Soon gas-masks were given out to everyone, and we were supposed to practise using them. We didn't do much of this, but mercifully we never needed them. To encourage small children to put them on, instead of the frightening black rubber, their masks were coloured and made to resemble Micky Mouse. Simon had one of these but I don't think we ever managed to get it on him. For babies there was a terrifying (to us) box in which mothers had to put the whole baby and pump with filtered air. Mother could hardly bear to look at it. The whole lot, masks and box, were packed away into a cupboard near the front door, so that they were out of sight yet near at hand if needed. We never wore them over our shoulders in the special cases made for the purpose, as so many children had to do as they set off for school each day. Happily for us, school was home.

Simon and Bridget, aged 8 and 5

The Litchfield family 1947

chapter seven

Light amid shadows

Because I remember so much of those war-time years, it's hard to know which memories to pick out, and which to let slip away into the mists. Everyone who lived through that time will have many very clear pictures, but we will all have different ones. Time is like that – Gerard Manley Hopkins put it so profoundly when he said, 'Vastness blurs and time beats level'.

One of the first things Bou and I had to do was to take down all the iron crosses and swastikas we had crayoned on large pieces of paper and hung up in the windows. For us there was nothing political intended. Germany was the home of many of our beloved composers, so we were mad about anything German. It was all right before the hostilities began; but Father had to point out to us very seriously that he, or we, might be arrested and put into prison if we didn't take them down TODAY. We did so, but reluctantly – children hate being told that they have *got* to do something, and normally our parents were very good at not making this mistake. They usually let us do our own thing, or were able to steer us gently and unobtrusively in the direction they saw was best.

It was not long before the air-raids started. Looking back, I marvel at how calmly everyone took them, and the matter-of-fact, practical way people coped. We would hear the wail of the siren, so often around seven or eight in the evening, and know that the enemy planes would soon be passing over. For us, in the depths of the countryside, there was always the presumption that they would be passing over – though we well knew that they might jettison their load of high-explosive bombs anywhere if attacked, before heading for home. Our hearts ached as we thought of the people in the cities they were actually making for. But we had our little procedure, at any rate at the beginning of the war. As it went on, everyone became more used to it, and took fewer precautions. If we had already gone to bed when the siren sounded we would get up, pick up our 'air-raid bundles' and go downstairs in our dressing-gowns to the living-room. These bundles were something people were encouraged to make – a little collection of things they might need when in an air-raid shelter, so that they didn't suddenly decide to rush back and get some vital requisite. I always took my knitting-bag in my bundle, having heard that knitting was recommended as soothing to the nerves!

We could hear the steady drone of the enemy planes overhead, and not infrequently the WUMP, WUMP of distant bombs exploding. The vibration could be felt even from miles away, and crockery on our shelves would shake. If the thuds seemed nearer than usual, we children would go behind the piano or get under the table, feeling safer in its protection. Our parents sat in their chairs by the embers of the fire – strangely, I can't remember what we did with the baby and little Simon: probably one was put into the pram and the other slept on the settee. Bou and I didn't attempt to rest. We knitted or sewed or talked together quietly, aware as far as our understanding at that age could take it in of the danger, yet mercifully too young to see the horror of the whole situation. I don't remember being really frightened; but perhaps the years of peace have dulled the sharpness of the memory.

Our lives continued to follow the daily rhythm of lessons and play, mostly out of doors. Always there were books to be read, and so much to be done that the days were never long enough. On the light summer evenings it was hard to go to bed. We would watch the hay-waggons being pulled up the lane by two big cart-horses, one behind the other – no one today knows how those hay-waggons looked, or their wonderful fragrance. There were no bales then, just the loose hay piled expertly onto the huge wooden waggons to a great height, as farmers had done for centuries. The lane was narrow, and the corner of our coal shed jutted out a bit, sometimes catching a wisp of hay and pulling it from the side of the waggon. After the horses had plodded their steady way up to the farm, we would run out and gather up the sweet-smelling hay for our rabbit hutch. If the weather was right, and particularly if there was the possibility of rain coming soon, which those men of the land knew well how to foretell, they would work long and late to

48

get the precious harvest of hay safely home before it was spoilt. Once back in the rick-yard it was stacked and thatched, another craft in itself. A thatcher was always assured of work, particularly in the summer and autumn, and there were two or three in the village. Alby Norton used to make spars out of withy and other strong, supple striplings of wood to fix down the thatch; these were like giant wooden hairpins. Making them was yet another craft, one that is probably almost extinct now.

Each season had its highlights, its own special scents and sounds. Autumn was filled with the fruits of the earth: the corn being cut in the fields; swedes and mangel-worzels being lifted and brought to the farms, where they were piled in clamps. These were large mounds of roots covered with straw and then earth, and smoothed over so that most of the rain ran off. The roots kept well all the winter for animal feed. We used to get hold of a swede or two when visiting the nearby farm, wipe off any excess mud on the lining of our coats (where we thought it would not be seen), grate off the thick skin with our teeth, and then munch away.

The war put more urgency into all these harvesting operations. They had gone on more or less unchangingly for hundreds of years, although by that time most farmers were no longer cutting hay or corn by hand. Horse-drawn implements were being used on all our nearest farms, and represented a great step forward towards the mechanization we take for granted today. Now the whole country was engaged in the war effort, saving and using every scrap of food and sharing with their neighbours. Everything that could be grown at home saved valuable ships, manpower, time and money. The nation had to be kept fed and healthy with the mininum of imported foodstuffs. 'Dig for Victory' was one of the many slogans of the day, and people set to with a will to grow all they could. Patches of hitherto unused ground were dug and planted, and many a flower bed was turned into a vegetable plot. Children and adults scoured the woods and hedgerows for wild fruits. Blackberries, rosehips, crab-apples, elderberries, sloes – everything that could be eaten was eagerly gathered in and turned into jam, syrup, chutney or bottled fruit for the lean days of winter. People forgot about the little differences and quarrels amongst themselves as they worked together to win this war against a common enemy. It made me feel sad that once peace returned the spirit of comradeship faded to a great extent and the old bickerings were resumed.

Winters could be very cold. Houses were not centrally heated – were not in fact heated at all. The living-room would have its fire and once that was lit there was one warm room; the kitchen became warm while the cooking was being done. But there was no attempt at heating the other downstairs rooms or upstairs. If there was a new baby, or we were ill, Mother would light the old black Valor stove and bring it into our bedrooms for a while to give a little warmth as we undressed. Its light made exciting patterns on the ceiling of the dark bedroom. Although there were electric lights in the bedrooms, we could not afford bulbs most of the time. And in the war years there was no chance of using electric lights unless one had very meticulous arrangements for blacking out the windows, which we did not have. Even a tiny chink of light showing from the lane would bring an Air Raid Warden to the door. The living-room had shutters, and in the kitchen it was quite easy to hang a blanket or an old coat over the window, so these rooms could be well lit. Tiny oil-lamps had to suffice for the hallway and bedrooms. I marvel now how we didn't have accidents in the dark as we went up and down the twisted stairway, with its steps narrowing to nothing as it rounded the corner.

Most of the downstairs rooms had stone floors – beautiful but often uneven grey flagstones. Here and there we had mats. Mother always liked to have one under the kitchen table, where we had our meals, as she thought it could cause rheumatism if we sat with our feet on the stone floor for any length of time. Fortunately, none of us sat still anywhere for very long. The energy of youth kept us bouncing around and usually warm, though I do remember feeling very cold at times.

But winter brought Christmas. It says so much for the way our parents used everything for our pleasure and our good that our awareness of the mystery of Christmas became so deeply embedded in our lives. Money may have been scarce in our house, but we had wealth in abundance of the things that money cannot buy – above all, lots of love.

50

We had a small crib which we put up every year. Even that was poor, in that it lacked the main figures of Mary and Joseph. But there were several kings (certainly more than three, two of them identical twins!), some shepherds, a number of sheep, the ox and ass, and a few other animals that somehow got in. It was always a great day when we got the crib out from its box in the hall cupboard, and many were the squeals of delight as we met again the familiar characters of the Christmas story. Even the dried moss was packed away every year and came out again looking good as new; and the little stable, made of wood, stood up bravely to the strain of the somewhat rough handling of eager children all wanting to arrange it themselves.

The crib was usually the first thing to come out during those exciting days leading up to Christmas – in fact it was put up when Mother could no longer withstand the anguished: 'When can we start putting up the Christmas things?' Next, there were the paper-chains to make. Strips of coloured paper could be bought for the purpose, only costing a few pence but worth their weight in gold for parents. A packet of these papers and a cup of flour-and-water paste kept children reasonably quiet for an hour or more. The fact that the completed paper-chains, the furniture, our clothes, and the surrounding floor became splattered all over with white, dried-on paste, dimmed neither the thrill for us nor, apparently, our parents' pleasure. They hung up the wiggly, floury chains with pride, and much consideration of where they would look the most beautiful.

Father also loved festoons, the kind he had seen in churches abroad, so for several years we made these too, with little sprigs of bay from the large bush that sheltered against the front wall of the house. We tied these along pieces of string and Father put them up across the length of the front room where they looked lovely – to begin with. After a while they withered and our tying came undone. We didn't know as much then as we do now about making garlands; but we loved the fragrance of those bay-leaf festoons. When we took the decorations down, we would give the festoons to our goats to eat. I think they must have eaten the string as well and they, too, smelled of bay for hours afterwards. They

51

were not milking goats, just two entertaining pets we kept for a few years.

Christmas lists had to be written in good time, and solemnly put up the chimney for Father Christmas. Our choice of presents was skilfully yet unobtrusively guided: it was *no* use asking him for a bicycle (my perennial moan!) for how could Father Christmas possibly get such expensive presents for all the children he visited? Why not ask for something like . . . ? I don't know how they worked it all out, for there were certainly no shopping sprees before Christmas. All through the year Mother kept her eyes open for bargains, her ears for the things we wished we had, spending a few pence here and there, and by Christmas Eve would have our stockings full of what we hailed as treasures. One had to try to be very good during those last days before Christmas: Father Christmas had a way of finding out who had been naughty and might well stay his lavish hand when the time came for filling one's stocking.

The tree was the last thing to be put up. Sometimes we had a live one, or a branch of fir or pine picked up on a walk, but latterly we had a little fold-up artificial one. It must have been quite dangerous with its candles in clip-on tin holders, its cotton-wool snow along the branches, bits of tinsel, a few baubles and glass birds and some very small gifts tied to the branches. But we never left it unattended when the candles were lit. How we loved our tree! And how our parents loved to watch our shining eyes as we gazed in wonder at what was in fact so simple a creation!

We didn't go to church at Christmas in the days when we were all little. Although there was a church in the village, and a Methodist chapel, we were not allowed to attend these because we were Catholics. This was before ecumenism was taken seriously – or even mentioned, in fact. Our own nearest church was at Glastonbury, five miles away, too far to walk; but we imbibed the story of the first Christmas as Mother played the piano and we sang many carols. Father would put in what he called 'the men's part'. He had a lovely tenor voice and the gift of being able to sing parts to any of the tunes. As some had better musical settings than others, he would arrange for Mother to play from the appropriate book. Suddenly he would exclaim: 'You're not singing, Mum!'

'I don't know either the words or the music by heart', she had to reply. 'And I can't read both at once!'

'But of course you must sing!' I think he loved to hear her voice, which was also very true and sweet. When he was older, Simon would join in the accompaniment on his violin.

Over those last days as Christmas approached, we sat with our paintboxes and crayons, and drew and coloured our Christmas cards. These were sent off proudly to our grandparents and aunts and uncles – I don't think we ever bought any. We understood that our own creations meant much more to our loved ones.

The postman coming to our own door, too, was part of the growing excitement. By today's standards we didn't receive many cards, but the few that did arrive gave us great delight. They were nearly always embellished with a bow of bright ribbon or cord, and we put them up as part of the decorations. Sometimes the postman even brought a parcel – what eagerness, as we all crowded round to get the first peep at what was inside! It didn't really matter too much what it was – it was the fact that a parcel had come that gave us such pleasure. The postman delivered all the mail, twice a day, all over the long and straggling village, on his push-bike, come rain, come shine - and always with a cheery smile.

We had no holly in the garden but plenty of ivy, so this was gathered to put behind the pictures and along any available ledge. Somerset was mistletoe country – we did have some on one of our own apple trees, but it was stolen during the early war years. However, Father usually managed to get a sprig from somewhere to hang in a conspicuous place.

On Christmas Eve came the long awaited choosing of some of Mother's old stockings, labelling them with our names, and hanging them over the fender. There was always a high wire fender round the fireplace all the time we had a baby or small child in the house, to avoid the possibility of accidents; it was more often than not draped with drying nappies and other garments. There were no airing cupboards or other source of heat for this purpose. We always left a mince-pie in an obvious place for Father Christmas to nibble as he filled our stockings. Somehow he managed to get them upstairs to where we lay fast asleep. And how very early we awakened on that most special morning of the year! The squeals of delight must have disturbed parents who perhaps felt as if they had only just got off to bed! We would run into their room and show Mother the wonderful gifts – I can see her face now, lit up with pleasure as if she were seeing the toys for the very first time. I thought her joy was for the same reason as ours, but I realise now that her joy came from seeing ours. She would puzzle with us over the instructions as to how a thing worked, and we thought how clever she was to pick them up so quickly, not knowing that she'd read it all beforehand! Father, meanwhile, had slipped away to go downstairs and put the kettle on. This was his job every day of the year. The first sound of which we were conscious each morning was the creak of the step down from their bedroom: Dad going downstairs – soon the tea would come up. He used to try to creep down the twisty stairs, but that one creaking step always gave him away.

All our growing years we were lucky enough to have not only our first morning cup of tea brought to us in bed, but also our breakfast not long afterwards, and even more tea if we liked. Father would also bring up any post that had come for us, and the morning paper for Mother to have a quick glance at, if it came in time. How he did all this with only one arm seems amazing to me now but at the time we did not give it a thought. He liked to provide the first meal of the day and I believe he liked to be the first one around, and to see what post had come. He always took special care over Mother's cup of tea and breakfast; he wanted them to be just right. They were still, always, so much in love. It must have given Mother a good start to the busy day that lay ahead of her.

Our Christmas fare was very meagre, compared with the ideas of today. Mother always made a Christmas pudding which was hailed with delight and ecstasy. In fact it was composed almost entirely of bread-crumbs (soaked in cold tea to make the pudding brown), a handful of dried fruit and suet and a little mixed spice. Likewise the mincemeat for the little pies was mainly grated apple, with a small amount of suet and dried fruit. We never had turkey or any kind of bird; the budget didn't run that far. But there were always Brussels sprouts from the garden, potatoes, and whatever meat we could afford. Sometimes it was only sausages. But it was the Christmas dinner, and seemed wonderful – it had a glory of its own. Apple sauce usually appeared, though not the pork to go with it; but it went well with sprouts, and we always had plenty of apples from the orchard. Apples were our main Christmas gift for our friends. We even sent some by post to our two grannies, together with some little thing we had made, like a needlebook or a pen-wiper. Remember pen-wipers? They were little pieces of cloth stitched together through the middle and embellished with a button or bead to cover the stitching. They disappeared when biros and fountain-pens took over, but were very useful when all pens had to be dipped in an ink-well, and you needed to wipe off the ink before putting them back on the tray or in a pencil case. It spoilt the nib if the ink was left on to dry each time. We always made one for Father's birthday, never realising that he could not really use it – you need two hands to hold a pen and wipe its nib! But he always seemed pleased when we presented it to him.

Christmas Day was spent playing with our new toys, reading our books and each other's, and munching the apples that had been carefully picked out to save for this day – Blenheim Orange usually, or sometimes the little russets from the tree close to the house. We knew each of our apple trees and the merits of their fruits in a very personal way. Mother liked to eat a Bramley long before it had become sweet enough for most of us. We sometimes listened to the Radio. Good Christmas programmes to cater for children and adults were provided; and we had all listened on Christmas Eve to the carols from King's College Chapel, Cambridge – always a very moving experience for Father.

Both our parents had great ingenuity. They thought of lots of things to make those days between Christmas Day and Twelfth Night special for us. On one of the days Mother somehow managed, despite the rationing, to make a little party, to which a few of our closest friends were invited. Father had a gift for organising games on these occasions, and everyone thoroughly enjoyed them – always the little ceremony of the guests taking off their hats and coats and hanging them in the hallway to begin with, and saying 'Thank you very much for having me' before they went home. These customs we, too, were carefully taught to observe when any other children invited us to their own parties. Before the war several families had them, but most didn't feel they could manage it once the rationing began. Our own mother was not easily put off – she knew the war could last a long time, and that we should never see those childhood Christmasses again. She was determined that life should be as normal as possible for us, and that we should have our Christmas joys. We recall them with pleasure and gratitude, to this day.

During the week of Christmas, at some point we had to sit down and write our thank you letters. This chore was not received with too much enthusiasm; but it was pointed out to us how important it was to express our thanks. If our sense of gratitude didn't rise so high, Mother would try another tactic – cupboard love: 'if you don't thank Auntie for that lovely book, she might think you didn't like it, and not send you one next year'. This usually had the desired effect, and we dipped our pens in the ink-pot and got the job done as quickly as possible. I have always been glad of this early training. Gratitude and appreciation are health-giving – they seem to me to be gifts in themselves.

Then, when the twelve days of Christmas had come to an end, all the little crib figures were carefully and almost reverently packed away again in their box, along with the glass bird, the baubles and the little tin candleholders from the tree. Even the fragments of tinsel were saved; no tinsel could be had, all those war years, nor for a long while afterwards. Everything was put away for next year – and how very long a whole year seems, to a child! In later life, I've heard people decry tinsel and baubles, as if in some way they detract by their very glitter and simpleness from the true message of Christmas. For me, this could never be so. The flimsiest wisp of tinsel catching the sparkles of light and turning them into stars cries out to me the message of joy, and brings the Christmas story as surely to my mind and heart as even the greatest painting of the scene could do.

chapter eight

Living through war

It never ceases to amaze me how people can continue to live normal lives in spite of most abnormal and often terrible circumstances. There must be a built-in toughness in human nature that we don't reckon on when life is easier. The years of the war were not easy ones – to put it mildly – yet we all carried on, pulled together, sang a little song, and counted our blessings. Food rationing became more and more stringent, and sometimes even the rationed food was not available. In fact, the rationing was not as much of a hardship for our family as it was for many others, for the simple reason that we were accustomed to living frugally. Everything was on coupons or 'points', but it was more the shortage of cash that curtailed our food-buying. However, Mother was clever at managing, and at making nourishing meals for her brood out of unpromising provisions. She was before her time in realising the value of pulses, and potatoes were usually available at a reasonable price, after the delicious, home-grown 'first earlies' were finished. We were well content with a baked potato for our dinner. We hardly ever bought sweets, so could give away our sweet coupons, and clothing coupons too we sometimes passed on to other people. Mother was a good needlewoman. Her own mother had been a trained and highly-skilled dressmaker, even making men's overcoats. Mother didn't pretend to be an expert, but she could cut down old jackets and trousers and make children's wear from them; she also turned things inside out and made them up on the other side. One of the war-time slogans was 'make do and mend' and she certainly fulfilled this injunction to the letter. She was helped by gifts of passed-on clothing. Father had friends from his Cambridge days who still kept in touch; they had children a little older than we were, who went to boarding school and had very good clothes. Their parcels arrived at our house now and again and were always hailed with glee by Bou and me, and no doubt a certain relief by Mother.

Aunt Lucy helped, too. She spent all her working life doing secretarial work for the John Lewis Partnership, where Father had also been employed for a short while. She kept her eyes open for children's clothes and sometimes toys that hadn't sold and had been reduced in price. So a parcel arrived from her sometimes. Parcels were always tied up with string and then secured with sealing-wax over the knots. There was no sellotape, of course, or other sticky packaging – even letters often had a blob of sealing-wax on the back. If one had a personal seal, this would be stamped on the wax while it was hot. Father used sealing-wax a lot, but just used the base of the ink bottle to smooth it out. I never see it now so I suppose it has been superseded by staples and sticky tape.

Later in the war the Red Cross and other charities opened exchange centres for children's clothing, again working on a system of 'points'. You took in some of your own children's clothes, providing they were in good condition, and were awarded so many points for each garment. With these you could acquire other clothes, according to your present needs. Sometimes there were new garments, like jumpers and other hand-knitted items that had been made by school-children and various other well-wishers for distribution by the Red Cross. A lot of these had been made in the USA to send to children in war-torn countries. One little dress that Mother brought back for Bridget had a note pinned inside the pocket from a schoolgirl in America, addressed to 'the little English girl who gets this dress'. Bridget herself wasn't old enough to write back, but one of the family did, because the address was on the note. A few letters were exchanged, but the correspondence fizzled out after a while.

Toys virtually disappeared from the shops. Simon had a toy farm with little lead models of animals, fences, waggons, farmer etc., all made perfectly to scale, with which he played endlessly when the days were too wet or dark to go on the real farm. I think these must have been bought one at a time, before or just at the beginning of the war. Any toy that keeps a child happy and reasonably quiet for hours at a time is well worth having, and these proved to be an excellent investment! Simon used to build little hay-ricks with tiny tufts of cotton-wool, and painstakingly load carts with plasticine mangolds. Before long toy-shops disappeared from the nearby towns, and were used for other purposes.

All the same, children were not entirely without playthings. A man in our road was clever with his hands and a craftsman with scraps of wood. He made wooden toys – push-along horses, hobby-horses, dolls' push-chairs, and pull-along bunnies. This last item was an invention of his own. It had four small wheels underneath, the front two on a bent axle, so that as the child pulled it along on a string it moved up and down. When we bought one from him, he explained, 'it de hop about, like!', his face shining with satisfaction and delight at our appreciation of his creativity. That became another family saying in our house: 'it de hop about, like'.

'Like' was used a lot in Ashcott as the last word of most sentences. If they did not end in 'like' they generally ended in a word that can only be spelt 's'n'. We couldn't make out at first what that meant, but later realised it was an abbreviated form of 'thou knowest' which became 'thees know' and then 's'n', meaning 'you know'. 'De' came into most sentences before a verb, meaning 'do' or 'does', e.g. 'he de come round Saturdays' meant 'he comes round on Saturdays'. Speaking of the past, it became 'did' and replaced the past tense of the verb: 'he did live over Street', where we would have said 'he lived, or had lived, at Street'. We had to learn all these intricacies of speech gradually. 'Casn't' was a shortened form of 'canst thou not', or 'can't you?'. 'Thee', 'thou' and 'thy' were used more than 'you' among the locals. This old Wessex English is dying out now that the new generation are accustomed to hearing radio and television.

Rag dolls, furry toys, cloth animals made of old coats and skirts were all being made by mothers, grannies and aunts, and were much loved by the children. Bou had a great gift with her needle even as a little girl. She could pick up a scrap of material from the rag bag and cut out a shape with no pattern or guide of any kind. Before long, there on the hearth rug where she was sitting, would appear a lovely little toy horse, or rabbit, or perhaps a duck. One day Father took us to see a friend who worked at a fur-degreasing factory. We saw the piles of sheepskins in the yard and were shown the various processes by which the fur was cleaned and dyed. I have forgotten the techniques but I do remember that we brought back a big parcel of remnants of beautiful, coloured sheepskin. Bou was in her element with these, and in this case she did use paper patterns from a magazine. The thick leather skin was tough work for little hands to sew; but she managed, and obtained woodshavings from the carpenter to use as stuffing. There were no stringent regulations about what could be used to stuff toys with then – people had other and weightier things on their minds. Most people used old stockings or other cut-up clothing, unless one was lucky enough to live near a factory where flock could be bought cheaply. A few of Bou's toys actually went on to the oil-man's cart, to be sold. They were snapped up eagerly and she was given the money for them the following week. But she made them mainly for our own little ones, and the neighbours' children. I did not have her flair, but did do a little sewing. In the main I think I stuck to my knitting, and sometimes crochet.

Lots of our games needed no toys. They were 'pretend' games, shared by all the various children who were so often in and out of our home. What looked to adult eyes like the kitchen table with a big cloth draped over it, was to us a Bedouin tent where camels might be arriving any minute . . .

Now and again, especially when it was nearly Christmas, we put on amateur theatricals. We did plays, dances and recitations, spending more time working at the dressing-up than practising the actual performances. Often a play was inspired by and revolved around some piece of equipment, such as a large packing-box that could easily be turned into a cave with a little imagination. Our parents had to sit and watch the performance, and clap at the right moments; and sometimes neighbours would come to swell the audience. No one ever appeared to think that what we produced was silly, or ridiculous. They took it in the spirit in which it was meant, and we were sure they really enjoyed it. Simon, aged about six, once ran off the stage in the middle of his act crying out 'She's got my gee-gee!', as he saw his little sister had climbed onto his wooden horse at the back of the room. No one could ride on that horse without his express permission!

We spent quite a lot of time writing, too. I think we fancied ourselves as being a bit like the Brontës – at any rate, they fired our imaginations when we heard about them. Father bought the whole set of their works, including Mrs Gaskell's *Life,* from a second-hand book dealer, and as we got a little older we revelled in them. He bought a number of these sets of books; he regularly received the catalogues and it was one of the things he could not resist – even though he couldn't really afford it and we would have to go short in other areas. We wrote stories and poems, and I began writing letters at an early age. At one point we decided to produce a weekly magazine between us but we couldn't agree about the format or content. After squabbling about it, we came to the conclusion that we would write two separate magazines, one each.

Although Bou was almost two years younger than I, she was brighter and much more perceptive. I had to use my two years of extra size and experience in my effort to try to get even at times. In the case of the magazines I could see, even though I was biased, that hers was by far the better and more appealing. *The Weekly Dove,* illustrated, with a botanical page, an astronomy feature, and other attractive items was quite obviously the better buy – there were even competitions in it. Mine bore the ponderous title *The Authoresses Magazine,* and must have been as dull as its name, as I cannot recall a single thing that was in it. I realised, deep down, that I'd have done much better to join in with Bou, and share ideas as we shared most things, but I was too proud to admit it.

Our parents encouraged our writing habits. Maybe it was part of their educational plan, but I think in the main they enjoyed seeing what we had written, when they got the chance. Often we kept our work strictly secret and carefully hidden. What gave us added encouragement was membership of a Children's Corner in a newspaper. Every week Mother's parents sent her their local paper, the *Wellingborough News,* which was of great interest to her, as she had lived all her life in Wellingborough before her marriage, and knew the people and surrounding area well. There was a very good page for children in it, run by a man we were actually to meet in years to come. Because it was a local, not national paper, the competitions it ran each week had fewer entrants, so we quite often won a prize. Children could send in letters, poems, even short stories, and have the pleasure of seeing them appear in the paper. One could also obtain pen-pals and I and the pen-friend I met through the Children's Corner still correspond today, over fifty years later. Mother carefully cut out all our little writings and prize-winnings and stuck them into an exercise book. Here is the first verse of one of Bou's early poems, written when she was five:

> *It really was a dreadful thing*
> *One morning when I found*
> *A Leo lion in my bed*
> *Asleep, all safe and sound!*

Children could join the corner at any age, once they could read, but had to resign on their seventeenth birthday.

Of course, there were nowhere near as many publications on the market for children as there are today. Comics were considered to be rubbish, and not allowed when I was young, though as the years went by our parents relented and the younger children borrowed them from friends sometimes. Although we always had a daily paper and some periodicals, these were carefully chosen. When I was a little girl, we had *G.K.'s Weekly,* and I still recall my parents' sorrow when Chesterton died and this came to an end. In his younger days Father had known Chesterton, and he had a deep admiration for him. In fact the only books we ever heard him recommend to anyone were the *Father Brown* stories and Conan Doyle's *Sherlock Holmes* books. We used to tease him that he'd never read anything else written in English! He always seemed to be reading in another language, apart from books about cricket.

chapter nine

Where the wild flower grows

Spring comes early in Ashcott, sheltered as it is from the worst of the northerly winds. By February, if you know where to look, you can gather the first violets, deep purple ones with that unique perfume. The earliest often appear under the hedgerows at the sides of ditches, in the moist and partially shaded environment they love. Not long after, you may expect to see primroses on the banks by the roadsides, with catkins and pussy-willows bursting forth above them. Then the cowslips in the fields, cuckoo flowers in the boggy parts, and bluebells in the shade of the woods.

There was a small but lovely wood quite near to our house which could be reached by crossing Farmer Winslade's fields. I feel I should pay a little tribute here to this man, because in his quiet way he was a big influence on our lives, not so much by what he said as by what he didn't say. He farmed Charity Farm, so called by a philanthropist of days gone by who arranged that the rent was to benefit the poor of the village. Even today, as far as I know, £5 is given to all the over-sixties of the village at Christmastide.

When Simon had moved on from being a chubby toddler to a slender slip of a boy, one of his pals from a nearby house took him up to the farm one day. Here he met all the animals: the huge cart-horses with their gentle eyes, the cows and calves, pigs in a sty, hens, geese, and dogs and cats strolling around the farmyard and lane in freedom all day long. He fell in love with it all, and before long he was up at the farm every day to 'help Harold'. It says a lot for Farmer Winslade that he, and his brother who lived in and helped with the work, were always Harold and Alan to Simon, which at that time was not usual. The rest of us would have called him Mr Winslade, but Simon was on a different footing at the farm; he felt he was part of the team, and they accepted his presence with kindness. Doubtless Simon, like all children of that age, asked innumerable questions, and it is quite remarkable that the busy farmer never sent him away. He sometimes called him Snowball, because Simon's very fair hair used to bleach almost white in the summer sunshine. Soon my brother began to do little jobs to help around the farm. When the men set off to plough, or hay-make, or dig swedes, or whatever, there was Simon's little white head showing above the side of the waggon or bobbing alongside. For some time he earned himself a penny a week, or some walnuts in season, by taking Mrs Winslade's grocery book up to the village shop, to save her a journey. This meant a lot to him, and was carefully recorded in his diary that evening. Some of his diaries of those years are still extant, and we have all much enjoyed re-reading them over the years.

Once, when our parents had been to Street for some shopping, and were coming back through Walton on the bus, a herd of cows walking along in their usual leisurely way slowed down the bus, as not infrequently happened on those country roads. Mother looked out of the window and saw to her amazement that the cows, on their way home for milking, were Harold's and that they were being herded by their small son, helped only by a stick and a trusty dog! We were not allowed on the main roads at that age and they had imagined that he was safely playing up at the farm. Evidently Harold knew that he would manage the cows perfectly well, which of course he did. In any case, no traffic went at any speed past cows. Everyone understood that half-past three on a midwinter's day was just on milking-time. This was a fact of life, accepted and respected.

When we were all a bit older, we had very exciting chasing games, running across Harold's fields, leaving chalk arrows or other pre-arranged signs on gates and fences to indicate the way we'd taken. Several children would arrive at our home on Saturday mornings to join in the game of the day, and weather permitting, (which was nearly always as it took a lot to deter us!) we divided into two teams, and one left first to lay the trail. After a few minutes the rest set off in pursuit, over fields, through gaps in hedges, over streams, back through the farm-yard, and sometimes even back home again without being caught by the followers.

Often when the latter were hot on the heels of the first team it became necessary to hide. I once hid inside an empty barrel in a grain-shed and have never forgotten the awful feeling of hearing the pursuers come into the shed and start searching. Inside a barrel one has absolutely no means of escape but is completely trapped. I pictured them all peering down at me in my helpless state and wondered what they might do to me. So I rose up and gave myself away. However, usually it was great fun to remain undiscovered and listen to the voices of the pursuers fading into the distance, and then move on, running back another way to reach home first. These were simple pleasures but greatly enjoyed, and as we ran, or crept, or crawled through the undergrowth we learned to recognise most of the wild flowers and plants around us.

We were careful not to walk where there were growing crops – country children are trained about that from an early age. Even so, some farmers resented groups of children running wild through their property, chalking signs on their gates. One angry shout, or a waving stick, would have put us off forever; but Harold never minded. He loved children. Later on he and his wife had a long-awaited daughter of their own; but she was still very young by the time we had stopped the chasing games, and had moved on to other occupations. But we still went down across those fields sometimes, to reach the woods.

A little tradition sprang up of going there for a picnic around Easter-time. During the winter the land became very boggy in places, making access to the woods more difficult, but once the March winds had dried it up a bit and the tender new green of early spring began to clothe the bare hedges, we'd feel we could wait no longer, and some sunny day set forth. On the way across Harold's fields there was the single root of red cowslip, which we looked for every year. There were always carpets of the lovely yellow ones, but only this one plant that put forth a red bloom. The primroses would be out by then, too, growing in tussocks along the sunny sides of the hedges. Once in the woods we were in a sea of bluebells, so thick that even the smallest foot could not tread without crushing some. There were wood-anemones there, too. It was like fairy-land, and we loved it all.

Bou became very knowledgeable about wild flowers; she had loved botany from a very early age. I knew the more obvious plants, but had to ask her the names of those we saw less often – and then would forget them again. Father too loved them all and would encourage us to find out not only their names but the families of the plants. Herbicides and pesticides were unheard of, so wild flowers grew in profusion, and children could pick as many as their hands and arms could carry.

On Sunday mornings for a number of years – certainly throughout the war – Father took us for a long walk. Sunday was also bath day, so before this took place we each had our weekly bath. Once we had all had our breakfast brought up to us and were reclining in bed reading our books – one of Father's rather clever and certainly innovative ways of teaching – he would put the kettle back on the stove. Then he would bring into the kitchen, which was warm by now, the oval zinc bath-tub. It was only a little domestic kettle, but when the water was boiling he would add it to a small amount of cold water in the tub, then go to the bottom of the stairs and give one 'bong' on the gong that hung in the hall. I was number one, so that was my signal to come down for my bath. So I got clean water, but only an inch or two of it, and I had to fold my knees up under my chin to fit myself in. While I was getting scrubbed, the kettle was put on again and when I hopped out Father would sound two on the gong, add the new water to the previous lot and Bou would come down for her turn. And so on for the third, fourth and fifth. By that time I would be dressed and ready to rub the knees and necks of the smaller ones. The last one had lovely deep water in comparison with the first, but by then it was decidedly opaque!

Somehow we all emerged bright and clean as new pins, and towels and other items were put into the same water for a wash. One has to remember that all water was precious, because it had to be carried right across the courtyard from the tap, and warm water doubly valuable, so we got every bit of use out of it. Finally it was carried back outside and put on the garden.

After the bathing was over and we were dressed in our clean Sunday clothes, Father took us for what came to be called the

66

Sunday walk and turned into a much-loved custom. We would set out, not knowing at first which way we would go. If the ground was wet we kept to the roads and lanes, but on the drier summer and autumn days we went up into the hills and maybe the woods. It was an ideal place for walking, providing one didn't mind a fair amount of climbing. Pedwell Hill was one of our favourite haunts. Pedwell itself was only a hamlet; Frances Ridley Havergal, the nineteenth century writer, had lived in one of the houses there in days gone by. The hill rose beside it, and stretched all the way along to Butleigh Monument and beyond. The lower slopes sometimes had cattle grazing on them, but higher up, where it was too steep, everything was wild and full of interesting things. Rabbits played there, birds of many kinds could be seen, and blackberries grew in abundance. Father had a keen eye for the first mushrooms – they were one of the things he spotted before we did; but we got to know the likely places for them. Old Man's Beard climbed up into the hawthorn bushes, and there were hazel nuts to gather in the autumn. But most of the time we didn't pick anything, just walked and explored and drank in the views from the highest points of the hill. Each season had its own beauty, and the hill was always new and different in its seasonal dress, yet in another sense always the same.

Sometimes we went to Loxley Woods, the last remnant of an ancient wood with some fine old trees. It is now not much more than a strip on either side of the main road, but it still possesses a grandeur that other patches of random woodland lack, though they all have a beauty of their own, and a character. Or we would stay on the lanes and walk round to Shapwick, the next village. From the top of Ashcott village one could see for many miles – Shapwick not far below and beyond was Brent Knoll, the sweep of the Mendips, Wells and Glastonbury, with the Tor watching over it all. On the clearest days, Steep Holm, the rock rising out of the sea which had become a bird sanctuary, could be seen; and a white wispy trail on the far-away hills – this was the steam from a train actually in Wales. All trains were steam-powered at that time.

There was always a mysterious beauty that was unique down on the peat moor, where the small, carefully-built stacks of peat stood between the rhines from which they had been cut. The turves had to dry out before they were ready for burning. Peat-cutting was all done by hand, and was the means of livelihood for a number of families. The flora was quite different on the moor – bog-cotton and bulrushes abounded, and yellow flag irises, and many more revellers in peaty, boggy land. There were few houses, often not a single one for miles. The rare cottages must have been very isolated in those days of no telephones or television. There were some telephones about, of course, but not in ordinary houses. Sometimes we walked as far as Sharpham and once we went on until we reached Glastonbury. The moor was a world apart, its secrets not easily divulged. We loved it, but I would not have wanted to wander there all alone. Perhaps I didn't really know it well enough to feel secure in its company. The moor on that side of the Poldens differed in character from Sedgemoor on the other side, looking towards the Quantocks. Though they had a lot in common, there were marked differences.

Sedgemoor did not have the primeval wildness of Sharpham and Shapwick, or 'peat moor'. It bore more marks of man's engineering. You could get a spectacular view of its layout from the top of the hill going towards Butleigh – past the Pipers Inn and on up Berhill until just beyond the windmill. The windmill no longer had sails but was a splendid stone-built tower-mill which had become a dwelling house. How we wished we lived there! Once you reached the crest of the hill, you could stand a little off the road, where the land fell away quite sharply. There before your eyes was spread the breath-taking panorama of Sedgemoor. No photograph could ever capture the extraordinary power of this view – either you would have to take it from the air, which would render the details too small to see, or you could only take a fraction at a time.

Someone might say – well, a whole area of absolute flatness, with some hills in the distance, what's so splendid in that? Once they had seen it, they would have understood. There is a timelessness about this view as you look down on the patterns of the fields that have been wrested from the hands of the encroaching waters. Despite the drainage rhines, particularly the eighteen-foot rhine, or Kings Sedgemoor Drain, as it was called, which carried a good deal of the water off the land, many of the fields became waterlogged or even submerged in times of heavy rain. But with care, and the expertise of farmers who have managed the land for generations, some crops can be grown and cattle reared and fed. You look down on the different colours of the fields, with the straight lines of the rhines dividing them like lines of stitching on a patchwork quilt. Here and there a dark square of woodland contrasts with the green, yellow and brown of the fields.

Then there are the villages, each with its splendid old church, many of them famous for their towers – Somerset is *the* place to see early church towers, with their carvings, and other features. The grey stone of the churches, with the houses clustered around them, is clearly visible for many, many miles, even with the naked eye. It is surprising how many villages you can actually see from that one spot. To the right the moor stetches on beyond one's sight, but looking ahead the Quantocks rise in the distance, making a beautiful backcloth to the scene. So it must all have looked, down the centuries; so the men saw it as they hurried out with their axes and pitchforks to fight the Battle of Sedgemoor – the last battle fought on English soil. The willows beside the rhines would have been pollarded as they are now, and the fields of withies grown, only in larger numbers, for the making of baskets, hurdles and many other useful household items such as cradles and basket-chairs. A few craftsmen are still working at this today in the area, but really only to keep the skill alive, whereas not many years ago the willows brought in a livelihood for lots of families. The advent of plastic has had a dramatic effect on so many trades that used natural materials.

I think that looking across the moor from that height gave me one of my first glimpses of infinity, and therefore of eternity. In some mysterious way it was a glimpse of God. Children have these moments, just sometimes – not always realised at the time, but later remembered and recognised. It is an experience of the beyond, of the all-enveloping, of the Other.

I am told that all the 'peat moor' side has since been taken over by huge mechanical diggers, scraping up the precious peat with their grasping iron claws and putting it into bags by the thousand, for sale at garden centres. The hand-tools which the diggers used in my childhood were either thrown on the fire or arranged in museums, where no one knows quite what was their purpose. At first all this grieved me as I thought of the vanished crafts and the people who lived so close to the wild things of nature, for the peat moor would have made a wonderful nature reserve, especially for butterflies and moths, had anyone thought of it before the peat-gobblers pounced. But I came to understand that this is how things are – one civilization arises, thrives for a while, and then is replaced by another; and soon the earlier one is quite forgotten. Maybe when men first began digging peat in blocks with iron tools, the generation that had lived there before were aghast at such savagery. In fact, the time when the whole area was under water was not so very far back. The Romans built roads on wooden piles – still in use, straight as arrows across the flat moor in the slightly less watery areas. Whole villages were built on similiar constructions. The monks of Glastonbury Abbey fished in the area, for most of it was lakeland, and Glastonbury was the Isle of Avalon, or Tennyson's *Island Valley of Avilion.*

I realised, too, that all the shoppers, who go around garden centres, or explore garden magazines as they plan the future beauty of their own little plot of land, delight in these bags of peat and carry them home in triumph. Nature is still spreading her gifts with liberality, not now as turves to burn for warmth, but to be returned to the soil, replenishing what has been used from it to provide us with food for our sustenance and flowers for our pleasure. And when the peat has all been cleared away from the moor, the machines will move away, and it will be their turn to be melted down. Their owners will go to rest with their fathers, and their descendants will find new and perhaps even more wonderful uses for the moor. Or maybe it will lie apparently unused for years, while nature quietly executes her own plans for it, and a new burst of beauty, new flora and fauna, will delight new eyes. People will ask why it is called Peat Moor and the pundits will give long, intricate explanations, involving derivations from ancient words. And we won't be there to tell them.

chapter ten

Victory

A big event for the village was the coming of the evacuees. A school from London's east end arrived with their teacher, and homes and school had to be arranged for them. All houses were checked for size and number of occupants and if there was room for one or more children, you had to take them. Mother was relieved that her four counted as sufficient for one home! But everyone rallied to the need, and with the great spirit that the war brought out even in hitherto rather aloof people places were found for all. The village school did double duty, Ashcott children using it in the mornings and the Londoners in the afternoons.

It was fortunate for the evacuees that all were housed in the village or its immediate surrounds and met together at the school, because it must have been a terrible experience for children to find themselves in such a different setting from their London homes. Many had come from very deprived backgrounds. The local people tried hard to make them feel welcome, but it was all so strange. The fact that they had one another was the one constant in a totally alien world. But they too had their share of bravery, and I think most of them managed to cope. Some, indeed, made great friends with their host-families and returned after the war to stay with them for holidays. We made a few friends amongst them, though the opportunity for seeing them to speak to didn't often arise. We were rather cut off, with not going to the local school. A group of them started up a little feud with us, climbing up on our gate and taunting us. No doubt we did look a bit odd – Bou and I often ran out to play in the garden with our hair unplaited, hanging down in a tangled mass; we must have appeared to be cave-dwellers, or characters from pre-historic times. One day the ring-leader of this little group actually climbed over the paddock gate and advanced towards us threateningly. I was scared stiff – she was only a girl about my size but we hadn't bargained for this. Mind you, we deserved it: we had given them as good as we'd got in the calling-out match! As I was the eldest on our side, and there were other and smaller children in our garden who had come to play, I felt it incumbent on me to rise to the fight. I marched forward with fists at the ready, anticipating a struggle, quaking with fear inside. We approached each other with calculated steps, each eyeing her opponent carefully. Just as I was about to thump she did the unexpected, and I thought cowardly, thing – up came one foot, and she kicked me in the tummy. It wasn't a very hard kick and did me no physical harm; but it damaged my pride severely – I fled the battle. To our relief she did, too, when she heard my yell; and after that there were no more skirmishes. We got to know their names in time, and all was forgotten.

Meanwhile Bridget was growing into a bonny little girl with bright brown eyes, rosy cheeks and a dark complexion. We loved her. Father often called her the Queen; and in fact on May the first each year for those growing years we used to gather wild flowers to make a little circlet, and crown her Queen of the May. She looked forward to this each year; she used to get a small gift in honour of the occasion, and she would speak of 'my May Queen' rather as she did of 'my birthday'.

The rationing system was carefully planned so that small children were entitled to extra body-building foodstuffs. Under-fives had a green ration book, older children had blue ones, and adults buff. This assured, as far as possible, that the nation's growing children were provided with at least the basic provisions for healthy growth. On the green ration book could be obtained a regular supply of cod-liver oil – hated by all, but 'very good for you'. Concentrated orange-juice was also available on these books, for the price of a postage-stamp. It was a valuable source of vitamin C, and much more pleasant. Sometimes when a certain food was in short supply, a notice would go up in the shop window: 'Only on green ration books', so that the little ones would not be deprived; and everyone understood and respected this. Powdered milk, dried eggs, margarine instead of butter – these were facts of living; but with home-grown or local-grown fruit and vegetables little Bridget thrived, as did the rest of us.

The evacuees didn't stay very long – I can't remember how long; but they had all gone back to London before some of the worst bombing took place. Their coming had, however, not been without its message for Ashcott. Though none of us realised it at the time, the village was beginning to change. As the years passed, the change accelerated until the pre-war fabric had almost entirely disintegrated. Outside influences, from a rapidly-changing world, began to slip in. Just as the first World War had been the end of an era, so too was the second one, though in a different way.

I remember one hard day we all had to face. A notice went up on the village-green notice board that all iron fences, gates, and railings were required for making munitions, and would be removed. We were very anxious, because though we only had one little iron gate, at the end of the front path, it opened onto a flight of five steep steps down onto the road. If there were no gate, a toddler could be down those steps before anyone could rescue him or her. We hoped those concerned with the collection would appreciate our dilemma; but no, a big lorry came round the village, and the man took everyone's gate off its hinges and removed it, to make bombs. Our little gate went, too, and though most people in time made or bought wooden ones, we couldn't afford one. However, no one ever did fall down the steps.

There was a very frightening day when a bomber raid took place in broad daylight. We were all in the stone-flagged courtyard at the back of the house looking up into the blue sunlit sky, watching the bombers flying over, high up but clearly visible. Then suddenly there was the terrible whine of a falling high-explosive bomb. We ran frantically indoors, but then . . . nothing. Silence. For a long time we felt the explosion must come. But it didn't. Apparently the bomb had fallen in a field near the High Street but had not gone off. Experts came and rendered it safe; but it made us realise that we were vulnerable, despite our distance from any large town.

On another occasion, two oil-bombs fell in an orchard close by our house. These did go off, but because there was nothing nearby to ignite the oil, no fire ensued. The trees, hedges and lane were bespattered with oil, and bits of twisted metal from the bombs were scattered over a wide area. Children collected them as souvenirs – 'Ashcott's bombs' – and played with them.

At night, after dark, we would lean out of the bedroom windows and watch the long fingers of the searchlight beams criss-crossing and feeling about in the sky as they tried to locate planes overhead. We used to hope they would miss them. During the day and at night we often heard anti-aircraft guns but we presumed they were practising, and they probably were. Convoys of troops and equipment frequently went along the main road through the village – first a few soldiers on khaki-painted motor-bikes, then jeeps, followed by bigger vehicles, army lorries full of supplies and troops, and sometimes cruel-looking tanks trundling along our peaceful Somerset roads. We used to stand at the side of the road and watch, waving to the soldiers as children will, taking it all in and fascinated by it. We had heard Father speaking about 'his' war, so we were not unaware of the seriousness of the manoeuvres, though mercifully we could not understand the full horror of it.

Barrage balloons were another familiar war-time sight, not actually in Ashcott but not far away. These huge, silvery-grey monsters floated about, high enough to dissuade attack from low-flying aircraft. Nets were held between the balloons. They looked quite grotesque.

Once Father took Bou and me on a long walk to Weston Zoyland aerodrome, which was quite a busy war-time air base. We could see it from above when we walked along the top of the hills, and as we were very keen on planes at that time Father said we would try to walk there. No other transport was available. It was a long walk but we were able to go right onto the runways and look at a couple of planes. A Spitfire was standing there for inspection – I think it must have been some kind of an open day, unless the men in charge were very lenient, because they let us climb into it. Before we left we saw, in another part of the aerodrome, a bomber loaded with bombs; and we knew it was destined to wreak havoc on some innocent town or village. We walked away from it, weighed down with heavy thoughts, and began to go across the runway in the direction of home. Then we became aware of a red light flashing on and off urgently. We calmly looked around, wondering what it was all about, then suddenly directly over our heads swept in a landing plane. We hadn't known it was coming because of the speed of its approach, but of course the control-tower had, and was frantically trying to warn us of our danger. We left soon after that – it was one of those near-disasters that happen so quickly that we don't realise their magnitude at the time. Afterwards we knew how lucky we had been.

As Bou and I grew older, into our early teens, we began to take what we felt was a more active part in the war effort. We had already been helping on the domestic side with the growing and gathering of crops and wild fruit, but now the Government were taking new initiatives to acquire funds for the armed forces. Events were organised all over the country and everyone was asked to cooperate where and as they could. Some of the cities and towns put on ambitious ventures. People rose to the challenge and a lot of talent emerged. Songs were written, entertainments of various kinds produced, and imaginative ways thought out for getting cash. The villages hadn't as much to draw on in the way of expertise or wherewithal but had easily as much keenness and enthusiasm. There were three big fund-raising drives over the years – called 'Salute the Soldier Week', 'Warship Week', and 'Wings for Victory', to raise money for each of the armed forces in turn.

The event that affected our own family most was the Bring and Buy sale. This involved most of the village in some capacity or other. There was usually a dance in the village hall, even though most of the younger men and women were away in the forces, the music being played on the piano or, more grandly, by a small band. There were no discos then – they came much later. School children put on an afternoon entertainment of sketches and songs, with occasionally an adult taking part as a conjuror or ventriloquist. But both old and young came to the Bring and Buy. You brought anything you either wanted to get rid of or felt you could spare in the way of household goods, and bric-a-brac as well as things you had made especially for the occasion. A few housewives even managed, despite the meagre rations, to make and bring home bakery, which were of course snapped up at once. Many were the recipes that the enterprising cooks thought up for cakes without eggs, sometimes even without fat, and with the minimum of sugar. Anything was a treat that had with a little ingenuity been made to look appetizing and different.

Bou and I worked hard beforehand with our needles and bits of material scrounged from other people's rag-bags. Any kind of soft toy sold well, and lavender bags, and babies' bibs. We had a little stall of our own, and stood behind it when the great afternoon came, proudly selling our wares, and feeling we had done so much for the war effort when we came to hand in our takings. Well, we had. And often we didn't even have the penny or twopence required to buy ourselves a cup of tea or a little bun. It was hard work, but it was all fun, and that I think was one of the main fruits of those 'weeks'. I suppose a lot of money was raised, but that would have soon been spent. Of more lasting value was the working together towards a goal (every area had its own target) and the enjoyment of everyone who participated. Friendships were forged, people felt good, and made others feel good.

On one occasion an elderly lady who lived alone had nothing to give to the Bring and Buy, but wanting to contribute something – she was very patriotic – went into her garden and cut her whole lovely patch of hyacinths. It was springtime, and she had watched eagerly for them to bloom. That day, on an impulse, she cut them all, put them in a pail of water, and brought them to the Bring and Buy. Because people were on the look out more for necessities like edible goods, clothing and gifts rather than the luxury of cut flowers, nobody bought them. As we left the hall we saw them there, still in the pail. We came home, and told Father about it – he didn't come to these events, usually. Immediately, though he had no cash, he sent us back to get them, promising to send the money up later. When we got there, they had gone. We hurried to the lady's house, which was quite near, and found that someone else had had the same feelings and hurried back to buy them after all. I tell this reminiscence because it highlights the spirit of concern and sensitivity of so many ordinary people living together through a time of so much trial and uncertainty. In spite of the harshness, the brutality, the senselessness of war, there yet remained a delicacy of touch in human nature that could not be fractured.

One of us asked Father what was in the papers before the war. For there was nothing else in them all those years, except what was in some way connected with war, despite the fact that all information of any importance had to be kept secret. Even in advertisements the pictures were always of people in uniform. It was a question Father remembered ever after.

I could linger over many more memories of those war years; but it would make this book too long. Instead I must turn to that day for which we had all prayed, hoped and worked; many had fought, and many had died: Victory.

In the end, it really happened. The taut band of tension snapped, and everyone was free at last. A mighty surge of relief, untranslatable into words and impossible to describe to anyone who has never experienced it, swept through the land. Exteriorly, nothing had changed, apart from the fact that the air raid sirens were heard no more, and the black-out was ended. Rationing went on for almost as long again as it had already lasted. Everything was in as short supply as before. But oh, the lads came home demobbed, and the girls from the ATS and other services. Ashcott was complete again and everyone could celebrate. Families put out flags and bunting and "WELCOME HOME" signs outside their houses when they knew their dear ones would return. During the first World War the village had suffered heavy casualties. Unless my memory serves me false, I don't think we lost any of our men in this one. Some had been taken prisoner, and took longer to get back, but I think they all eventually came home.

There were parties, street by street, and lots of events – not this time to get money from people in order to make more weapons, but simply for joy. Everything was free, those who had any cash handing out prizes to the children when they won races, those who hadn't helping to collect tables together or lending cups, or at least a hand. There was relief and great happiness on every face. I know that for those elsewhere, who had lost one or more members of their families – and there were so very, very many – there must have been an even greater sense of loss as they witnessed the home-comings and reunions. That pain was all around us, and even those who were most energetic in the celebrations were aware of this other side – the price that had been paid.

I was nearly sixteen when VE Day brought peace in Europe, and not long past my birthday when Japan surrendered and we celebrated VJ Day; Bou was fourteen. Life was still just as curtailed by shortage of goods and of money as it had been, but by now we were getting quite clever at managing. Everybody still had to be. It was common practice to take an old, worn-out jumper or cardigan carefully to pieces, unpick the parts that were still good, wash the wool, and then knit it up into another garment. Fathers' worn trousers were cut down to make smaller ones for their sons; ladies' dresses made children's skirts or frocks; and even furnishing materials like cretonne and butter-muslin, which were not on coupons, were used to make clothing. In our house, if we needed something that cost money, we knew we would have to use our ingenuity to create it ourselves – or go without. But it took a lot to beat us! Making things out of next to nothing was a challenge and usually fun. We made rugs out of snipped-up rags – not elegant but long-lasting and serviceable. Nothing at all was wasted. Once in a while a rag-and-bone man still came round, as of yore. He paid a few pence for a bundle of rags, but we never had any bones for him. What few well-stewed bones we had finished with were eagerly snapped up by our dog, or someone else's.

Newspapers were never thrown away. They had several uses before being either composted or used as firelighters. A folded paper was always used as a chopping-board for vegetables; another as a stand for hot saucepans, and others for putting on the floor to soak up spilt washing water. They were used under mats and carpets to help keep the cold of the stone floors a little further from our feet; and of course they were always used as toilet paper. Toilet rolls were rarely seen – in fact, it would have been considered unpatriotic to use them. Even public conveniences only offered newspaper, cut ready into squares. Shops, too, were always glad of any spare papers to use as wrapping paper for their wares. When I see all the paper that is wasted today, and hear the few voices raised to try to tell people to save it, I remember those days. We knew well enough how to save and use every scrap of paper then. It is a skill that needs to be relearnt – possibly not quite to the same extent, but at least in moderation.

In spite of all this making and mending and all the work that had to be done, with no labour-saving devices whatsoever, not even an electric iron or kettle, life was not pressurised in Ashcott, or at any rate not in our own home. Looking back, I see how almost all the teaching our parents gave us was by example rather than in words. It stood us in good stead in later years. One thing Mother always did, and which most of the other housewives didn't do, as far as we knew, was that once the washing-up was done after the midday meal, she would have her own daily wash (we always washed in the kitchen), take off her morning, working frock, put on a pretty one, and then settle down with her book for the afternoon. Whenever there was any sunshine she'd sit in the sheltered, sun-trap courtyard at the back of the house. She loved the sun. In winter she would sit by the fire. She didn't get on with her sewing or mending – this she did in the evenings; there were always lots of socks to be darned and other garments to mend. The afternoon was for relaxing and she sat reading, maybe keeping an eye on the youngest child at the same time, but otherwise just sitting there quietly. I think this had a quite specific effect on us all. Father would usually be sitting down at that time too, but he never sat in the sun. He'd sit indoors even in beautiful weather. His outdoor time was when he was gardening, or walking. All this gave a tranquillity to the home, and a great sense of peace and contentment. As we grew older and spent less time in active play, we too would settle down with our books (I often had my knitting at the same time) and read, or think the long, long thoughts of youth.

Three sisters from Somerset with Mother (1949)

chapter eleven

No greater gift

The following year was a very eventful one for our family. Two things happened which changed all our lives quite dramatically. One was the arrival of a new baby, Julian, at the end of the year. The other was that Bou and I went to school.

Even when we were still quite small, as we passed the convent school at Glastonbury on the bus, Father would say to us: 'one day perhaps you will go to school there'. It must have been something he longed for us to do. Yet the shortage of money while he was still trying to pay for the house, and then the outbreak of war, had rendered the whole idea impracticable. Whilst raids were a constant hazard, he and Mother wanted us all to be together; and we were all very happy in the 'Litchfield School'. But now at last things were looking a little brighter. Also, the arrival in the village of a new headmaster for the local school may well have been a contributing factor to Father's decision to send us to school that year. This teacher and his family were Catholics, and we made great friends with them. When their little girl made her First Communion, Bou and I were invited to the party at the Convent which she attended, so we met some of the sisters and had our first introduction to the school. I am quite sure those sisters, after meeting us, prayed that we should go there. They knew that we were Catholics, yet did not appear at Church. They wouldn't have realised how impossible it was for people in the outlying villages to get there, especially those with children, so surmised that we were lapsed and needed to be helped back. I don't know all the ins and outs, but I do know that as the summer went on there was talk of schools, clothes, and all sorts of related things, yet no one ever said to us that we were actually going there. In the end we could bear the suspense no longer and Bou tackled Father head on. 'Look here, Dad', she said firmly, 'we want to know. Are we going to this school, or are we not?' This amused him highly.

'Ultimatum from Bou!' he exclaimed. He was smiling, yet proud of his daughter's forthright approach.

It must have galvanized him into action and settled his indecision. Mother's pregnancy would have been a factor against our going, because so much more would fall on her with two big girls, by now quite useful, out of the house. However, from then on it was a definite fact that we would be starting at the Convent in September. Father never regretted taking this step. In any case, it must have been now or never as far as I was concerned, because at seventeen I would already be one of the oldest girls in the school, and a little later I would have been too old to settle comfortably with the other pupils.

Our father wanted so much for us to love learning. He had a powerful intellect, a quick wit, and a greatness of heart and mind that knew no bounds. He was also a very humble man, in the sense that he never took offence – he was always big enough to see life in its proper perspective. He had the right kind of pride; by which I mean self-respect and the ability to see and share in the best in other people. He was certainly very proud of all his children – he thought us wonderful! – and of course proud of his wife.

He had been born and brought up in Cambridge and was baptized in Little St Mary's. His family were Anglicans. We never discovered just when he became a Catholic, but felt it was most probably during, or immediately after, World War One (always referred to as 'Dad's War' in our house, to distinguish it from the one we all lived through.) He had two brothers and a sister, but sadly the little girl died of TB when she was about twelve. He must always have been studious – he used to tell us, thinking to spur us on, how as a boy he would sit at the old marble washstand in the bedroom he shared with one of his brothers, studying Greek, while the other lads were playing games in the street below. We considered this commendable, if not actually peculiar, but not something we felt called upon to emulate.

We, too, had one of those old marble-topped washstands in the bedroom to use as a desk – you could pick them up reasonably at sales. When visitors came, they were completed by a jug and bowl, and matching soap dish, and put to their proper use. These sets were important articles of furniture before bathrooms came into fashion, and often the chamber-pot matched the jug and bowl. So guests were always provided with *en suite* facilities, though of a slightly different variety from today's contraptions, with their gurgling pipes and noisy cisterns. It was quieter and more poetic – and certainly more ecologically sound.

Once, after Bou and I had gone to bed, I had occasion to need the chamber-pot we shared. It must have been badly cracked, as were many of our household commodities, because when I sat on it that night, it broke. The contents ran down the sloping bedroom floor, through the cracks and into the hall below. We both hurried downstairs and went into the front room to tell our parents what had happened. They were sitting there quietly, and Mother was quite annoyed to see us. 'You must have been playing about!' she scolded. 'No – I only sat on it', I explained. They found it hard to believe at first, but then I realized that I was standing in something sticky. I looked down at my bare feet, and found they were in a little pool of blood on the linoleum. I must have been cut by the broken pot, but by such a sharp edge that I hadn't felt it. Mother fled into the kitchen – she couldn't bear the sight of blood, especially on her own children. Father had seen such a lot of it during his lifetime, so he always took command on such occasions. He gently helped me to lie down on my front, on the floor, and kneeling beside me, wiped away the blood with a piece of rag. I shall never forget the infinite tenderness with which he patched the large cut with his one hand, using pieces of sticking-plaster.

Mother came in again once I'd been patched up, and we went back to bed provided with an old paint-can to use until such time as we could afford to buy another chamber-pot!

But I was writing about Father and his early days, before that digression. He must have been a brilliant student, as well as a good sportsman. He used to tell us how when as a boy he had borrowed one of the very early bicycles from a friend. It had no free wheel – this was not developed until later – so when you went downhill you just lifted your feet off the pedals and let the machine take you, often at breakneck speed. I gather there were no brakes, either. On this day, he had gone hurtling down a steep hill on one of the roads in Cambridge and crashed into a wall at the bottom. He managed to pick himself up, his face streaming with blood, and walked home. He wasn't seriously hurt, but felt very sorry for himself. He went into the house to his mother, but she must have been up to her eyes, as mothers of three lively lads often are, and she just looked up and said, 'what *now,* great dink?' It wasn't that she wasn't a loving mother – he also had some lovely tales to tell about her – but that day it must have been the last straw!

At University he became much involved with rowing, and we had several photographs from those days adorning the walls of our house. We also had an oar which had been presented to him, inscribed with the names of the boat crew of which he had been cox. He made lifelong friends among his fellow undergraduates, and was obviously in his element.

He was very handsome by all accounts – tall, with a fine bearing, and much charm. His interests were wide, and he loved life, and above all, people. There he was, a young man in his early twenties, with everything that could be desired, apart from money; and then the war came. With typical generosity, he enlisted in the Devon Regiment – I don't know whether there was a special reason for this choice of regiment, or if things just worked out that way. His father died three weeks before he was sent to the front. As an officer, he had to lead his men to almost certain death in that most terrible of all those battles in Flanders: Passchendaele. The very name still strikes like a heavy weight on all who hear it and knew of it.

In October 1917, he was smashed by a shell. His right arm was completely shattered, and his legs had lumps of shrapnel in the thigh and calves. He was left among the innumerable dead and he lay there, unconscious at first. Later he came to and looked up, from where he lay in the stinking mud full of half-rotting pieces of human bodies that was Passchendaele. He saw the stars. He had always loved them. He knew them all by name, knew the moon and the names of its landscapes – he was a keen astronomer. By the position of the stars, he knew which way to drag himself along, until he was picked up and carried to safety.

He never lost consciousness again, or so he maintained. He remembered being on the hospital ship as they brought the wounded home to England – how the nurses had tried to get him to taste a little food or drink; but all he had craved was a lemon. He had lost so much blood.

He was in hospital for a very long time – over four years, though towards the end of that time he was intermittently back at Cambridge, coaching the rowing crews. The surgeons tried everything to restore the use of his right arm. They tried to transfer the tendons from one part to another – modern replacement surgery had not yet evolved. But too much of the bone had gone, and in the end everyone realised that his arm would never be of use again. He couldn't bear the thought of having it removed altogether, so he kept it – I think he felt he would look more normal with something in his sleeve, even though the hand and arm could no longer be used. While he was in hospital, a friend for whom he used to write letters came to visit him and the tables were turned as Michael wrote *his* letters for *him*.

He had to learn to write with his left hand – and indeed do everything with it. But he had great spirit. I marvel now that no bitterness or resentment ever touched his life because of his disability. He had fought for his country, and given his arm in order that we who came afterwards should live in peace, and he was proud to have shed his blood for his brothers. He had, indeed, laid down his life for them.

The doctors were able to get his legs right and in time they healed, which was a great blessing. After that war, probably more than after the second one when everyone had become more disillusioned, the wounded soldiers were hailed as heroes – as indeed they were – and much was made of them. Opportunities were open to them. I think it was during that time that Father studied Criminal Law, and gained a degree in it. He never spoke of those intervening years between the end of the war and his marriage to Mother, which was not until 1928. He certainly enjoyed doing a kind of Sherlock Holmes act by searching out apparent mysteries in village life! But I don't think he ever did any professional work in that line. I'm sure that if we'd asked him he would have told us; but when one is young one's parents' past seems so very far back, even when in reality it's only a few years. Now that I'd be so interested to know, there is no one left alive who knew him then. So it is all hidden in the mysterious plan of God for us all.

Ashcott life must have been hard for Father in some ways. He loved his garden, his family, his books, but there was little stimulation for so active a mind. It was probably because of this that he used to go down to the local pub – we called it the inn in those days – and sit there, talking to the locals, and imbibing the strong Somerset cider. It didn't take a lot of that to make anyone unsteady on their feet, and the result was that he sometimes took more than he realised. He didn't get bad-tempered – just different from his normal dear self. Of course, it didn't often happen. He never went to the pub on Sundays or days when we were doing something special at home; and usually when he did go he came home none the worse. I think he found it difficult to refuse – it was part of his great enjoyment of everything in life. It was something we never spoke about, as though by some deep, mutual agreement. At the time, I used to worry – I didn't understand. With hindsight I see further. While Father was always the strong protector and defender, and the rock of support for us all, he, too, was vulnerable and we in our turn needed to become a shield and ally in his times of weakness. We learned the first steps on the journey towards compassion, forbearance and forgiveness.

He was generous to a fault, and couldn't bear to see anyone in need, if there was something he could do about it. His war disablement pension was not increased as the family grew in size. We all knew that he could never have been rich – if anyone had given him a thousand pounds, he would soon have given it all away. He gave away his own clothes, even his only coat one cold winter, to the various men who slept rough around the farms – poor Mother found this quite difficult at times! But her love always triumphed whatever he did, even though it was she who had to worry about shoes for the children, and the growing bill at the grocer's. Somehow he always *did* manage – the bills ultimately got paid, and we always had a meal. He had good friends, and

86

borrowed quite often – no one could refuse him!

His visits to the Ashcott Inn were not without their fruits in other ways. Everyone who visited the village frequented it, and he met a lot of very interesting people, often quite famous ones. Some he would bring home and introduce to us all, and friendships began that have lasted the rest of our lives. He also loved the very poorest, who dossed down at night in disused farm buildings, and had no work or anyone to care for them. They occasionally earned a little by helping out the farmers at busy seasons, or they would snare a rabbit and sell it, or gather bunches of water-cress. They were hard hit by the rationing system; because most of them could not read, and had no address, they slipped through the government net. He helped them, stood up for their rights, and did all that lay in his power on their behalf. He really loved them all, and they in their turn respected and loved him. Sometimes he asked their advice about things they really knew about; he was always ready to learn. Once he took me with him to visit old George, whom he had heard was ill. He slept in a hayloft on one of the farms, and we climbed up a ladder into the loft. There lay George on a sort of camp-bed, with a blanket over him, and fleas crawling and hopping visibly around him.

Sometimes Father did a little coaching, but again he hated charging a fee. Other children would join us in the 'Litchfield School' for certain lessons, and once a little girl came every day for a while during a long visit to the village. Before he came to Somerset, he had had older students who came on a regular basis. Not so many of those were around in the Ashcott of that time, though all this was soon to change. One of his friends was starting what was then a new school, at Street. Millfield was within a few years to become internationally famous, but I remember two or three of its first teachers riding through the village on their bicycles in those early days.

We were so proud of Father and admired him greatly. He had a gift for organising events in the village; and he was a very able chairman when there were meetings. He enjoyed election campaigns, and so did we. For a while Bridgwater was fortunate in having an excellent MP in Vernon Bartlett. He came to our house a couple of times, so we felt we knew him – he could speak seven languages. Father used to chair the meetings prior to the elections, and I still recall the thrill when Vernon was elected.

It is because I had so loving a father that I have always found it so easy and natural to think of God as our Father – I know how much fathers love, and how endless is their patience, and when necessary, their forgiveness.

We have now reached September 1946, and Bou and I are about to begin a wholly new kind of life, as we pack our few belongings into a suit-case and set out for Glastonbury, to become pupils at the Convent boarding school.

chapter twelve

Into unknown territory

When we arrived at the school we were met by the nun who was to become one of our greatest friends until her death fifty years later. Sister Eugenie was at the time head-mistress, and also in charge of the boarders, so we saw a lot of her over the next year, although her special teaching skill was with the little ones. She was in her thirties, tall, graceful, alert, and very kind. Her blue eyes missed nothing that we did – good or bad – despite the stiff white 'blinkers' (as we called them) that were part of the nuns' habit in those days; but they were also full of fun, and of sensitivity. Sister welcomed us so warmly that we began to feel more comfortable, and we followed her up two flights of stairs to the top of the school building, where the dormitory was. The convent itself was a large 'gentleman's house' which had been converted, but the school was purpose-built adjoining it. The dormitory looked spacious and bare after home. But it was sunny and bright, with large windows, and the two rows of beds had white coverlets and each had a locker beside it. The floor was of polished wood, and the walls were cream. One corner was partitioned off into a little cubicle. This was Sister Eugenie's tiny room. The partition was not very high; I realised long afterwards that she must have had quite a hard time, with no real privacy and on call every night, should one of the children be unable to sleep or have other difficulties. She certainly gave all, day and night.

We put our few clean clothes and personal things into our lockers. Our beds were side by side, to our relief and comfort. We were shown the room next door, where all the wash-basins were. Then Sister said to me: 'Just take this mop, Marie, and mop over the floor round the beds'. I took the mop, and set to work; but the incident had a profound effect on me, unbeknown to her. I saw in a flash that this was going to be so very different from anything we had experienced before. No one had ever *told* us to work. We chose to do it, or were perhaps asked if we could or would. It was suggested sometimes, but never commanded. Although Sister's request was made in the kindest possible way, I knew we would have to be prepared to begin something quite new to us both.

Soon the other boarders arrived, and by the end of the following day the dormitory beds were nearly all occupied. There were only about a dozen boarders. The whole school had about a hundred pupils. As we were a small group, it was much more personal and family-like than we had feared, and we quickly felt at home with the other girls. One was about my age, the rest younger; the little one was only four years old.

I am told it has become quite fashionable today to criticise convent school education adversely. At first this saddened me, because my own time at school had been so happy, and brought with it many added benefits over and above the academic tuition for which I had been sent there. All the friends I made speak highly of their time with the sisters, and have nothing but praise and gratitude for it. Later I realised that it is no new thing for a child to dislike school – any school; Shakespeare's unwilling school-boy would have been by no means the first. One of my brothers was not happy at school, although he was deeply appreciative afterwards of all that he had gained there. Some plants will grow well in an environment that simply does not suit others. We are all so different, and our needs and expectations are unique to each one.

Bou and I were lucky in that we had each other, so we were not completely severed from the family. I felt then, and I still feel now, that it can't be a good thing for a little four-year-old to be sent away alone to a boarding school. Yet, if it is the only solution, the ones who go to a convent are better placed than others to learn those precious truths that we first come to know at our mother's knee. It has been my privilege to witness the tenderness and kindness of the sisters, as they helped their charges through the trauma and pain of having to be separated from those with whom they had lived before.

Most of the nuns were French, at the time I was there; but the ones who had most to do with us were English or Irish. I think

90

this was a little disappointing for Father – it said on the school prospectus that there would be 'excellent facilities for acquiring the French language'. He hoped that the nuns would succeed where he had somewhat failed in this part of our schooling. In fact, we never did try talking to anyone in French – the nuns had been long enough in England to be able to speak English fluently, so we just didn't make the effort to practise what we had been taught. This was one of my subsequent regrets.

We had wondered how we would fit in with school class-work – whether we would be behind other children of our age, or ahead of them. It was a relief to find that although we had not done as much learning by rote, we had covered most of the ground in nearly all subjects, and in some a good deal more. Ours had been a broader spectrum; we found the girls knew little of current affairs, and our friends the composers and writers were unknown to them. But we needed at first some extra tuition in catechetics – those were the days of learning the catechism by heart. The study of the whole Sacramental system opened up new vistas for us. Though we had always known we were Catholics, and knew a fair amount about the saints, as well as having read the Bible for many years, we didn't have much liturgical formation as regards Mass and other services. We knew plenty of hymns, and of course the carols, probably more than the others did, because there wasn't a lot of singing in Catholic churches at that time. But there was the Gregorian Chant, and this was for us a tremendous new experience. We took to it like ducks to water and looked forward to choir practice each week, when we prepared the singing for the High Mass on the following Sunday. Again it was Sister Eugenie who played the organ and was choir-mistress, among so many other jobs; and she was a good teacher. A little group of people from the parish came to these practices, which were held in the school; then on Sunday mornings we all went up into the choir-loft in the Church, and sang our hearts out, following the notes in the Plain Chant books with zest and excitement.

Saturday and Sunday were the best days of the week. On Saturday we wore our own clothes, instead of the gym-slips and blouses of weekdays. In the morning we had a mending session with Sister Aurelie, the small and delightful sister from Brittany who supervised our sewing. Most of us had socks to mend, or 'poppers' to sew on. Sister Aurelie looked at the clothes carefully, for it was she who saw to the washing and ironing. She would manage to find a hole in socks that we were convinced were still quite sound – we thought she might even have made some of them herself! She was a gifted needlewoman and liked to see our work well done; but she always had a helping hand for those who simply could not manage.

We were free to play or read for part of the time, though even weekends were fairly tightly structured. Usually Sister Eugenie took us out to do shopping at some point. A few of the girls had pocket-money, and liked to buy sweets; and we all enjoyed the walk up the town. We had to walk in 'crocodile' with Sister at the back so she could keep an eye on us. Occasionally we went to call on a parishioner if Sister had a message to deliver – she was a great one for fitting in jobs where possible, and telephones weren't in general use at that time.

On summer afternoons we'd play tennis – there was a good tennis-court, and the older girls liked a game, while the younger ones played on the swings. In the evening there would be homework, ready for the following week.

Sunday was different again. On that day we wore our Sunday uniform, a brown pinafore skirt with a yellow blouse, and we felt smart and rather special. Glastonbury had two very old Anglican churches, and though our own church did not have bells the other two did. One of my lasting memories of Sundays at school is of us sitting in one of the class-rooms writing our letters, and listening to the pealing of the bells.

On Sunday afternoons, if the weather was fine, we went for a really long walk, sometimes taking a book with us or a letter we wanted to write. Climbing the Tor was our greatest delight, and looking from the top on the whole panorama of the moors below. Then there was Bushy Combe, another beauty spot, and Wearyall Hill, where Joseph of Arimathea is said to have planted his staff: overnight the staff grew and burst into blossom, though it was Christmas Day. This was the first Glastonbury Thorn, which still blooms at that time of the year. A tradition sprang up in later years of sending a spray of the thorn to the Queen for Christmas Day – I believe this still goes on. Sometimes we just walked, but in hot weather we'd find a shady place under the trees and sit down to rest awhile, and perhaps read. We loved those walks – maybe for Bou and me it felt like a continuation of our own Sunday walks at home.

In the evening we all went to Benediction, and sang again in the choir. After that it was supper and bed-time. I was always sad to see Sunday come to an end. The class-room days were hard going, to me at any rate. I suppose it was because we had always been so free at home.

As winter came on, it became colder and colder. That particular winter was a record year for prolonged ice and snow, and very low temperatures. The nuns tried hard to warm the place for us – they kept a big boiler going in the cellar, which was supposed to heat radiators throughout the school building. But the system was huge and old-fashioned, and the rooms high, without carpets, and bare except for necessary furniture. There was a black Valor stove which was carried around to whichever room we were using at that time – refectory, recreation room, etc. – but because the temperature outside was so low it did little to warm us. We all found it very cold, and I began to get chilblains for the first time in my life. Looking back, I realise that we didn't wear enough clothes. The war-time garments were thin and not warm – nothing like all the cosy clothing that is available today. Somehow we never put on another jumper on top – perhaps because we thought we would look fat, or because it just wasn't done fashion-wise – but it would have helped. In later years I see what slaves we can all become to fashion and convention.

It seemed ages before half-term came, and we went home for a few days. How small the rooms now looked, by comparison with those dormitories and classrooms! Even though it was not heated, our bedroom seemed so cosy, with its familiar objects, and the clothes hanging on the back of the door. Our house boasted no wardrobes, but there were hooks on the door and walls, some in the corners with a curtain over to keep the dust off the garments.

Most of the underclothes spent their time airing on a string line across the kitchen. We didn't have many items each – one on, one off was the general quota, except for babies and small children.

After half-term, apart from the cold, things brightened up as we prepared for the Christmas concert and jumble sale. Along with a few others of my age group I was given extra time for study while the rest were practising, and I took no part in the concert – we were expected to put all our efforts into working for the exam we proposed to take the following summer. This was a bit of a disappointment for me; but I managed to share in helping with the costume and scenery preparation. Bou was always good at acting and her contribution was much appreciated. The concert was put on for an afternoon and an evening, and brought in a little money for the nuns.

How they managed financially is difficult to fathom – mainly it must have been the sheer hard work of each of the sisters. The fees they charged were very low – though I think they scaled them a bit to fit the circumstances. A poor family was charged very little so that their children could be given a Catholic education and taught their faith, as happened in our case. They paid several lay teachers; our form mistress was one, a pleasant Irish lady whom we thought quite old, though she must have been only thirty, if that! The sisters were thrifty, growing vegetables and fruit, milking their own cow and doing all the cooking and bakery themselves, apart from bread and an occasional cake. In years gone by they had taken in laundry. They had had an orphanage, and trained some of the girls in laundry-work. By the time we were there all that had finished, but the laundry at the far end of the garden was in regular use for all the needs of the convent, school, and adjoining church. It would be a museum if still there today – coppers fuelled by wood or coal, a round, closed-in stove with places for heating several flat-irons at a time, and racks for drying. The only use of electricity was for lighting, and even this would have been a recent acquisition. They certainly knew how to wash – the sacristy linen was a joy to see, and even our unpretentious pyjamas and nighties came back from the wash folded and pressed as if they were brand new.

Each sister had her task, or rather many tasks, and gave herself to them with wholehearted zeal and an infectious joy. All her work was done for love – love of the God whom she had been called to serve, and love of those in whose persons she served Him. In fact, I saw afterwards that this was one of the main lessons I learned during my year as a pupil at the convent. I saw that happiness doesn't consist in having much but in loving much, and in knowing that we are loved.

We had gone to school ostensibly to experience another kind of studying and to take an exam or two. What we actually learned was something unique. Maybe it was what Father really hoped we would learn when he sent us there – though I know he also wanted us to follow in his own footsteps, and go to Cambridge. He wanted that for each of us, so very much. But we were an obstinate, independent bunch of individuals, and preferred to go our own way. In the end only Julian went to Cambridge, to Fitzwilliam College where Father had studied. While this gave Father immense joy, I don't think he begrudged us following the paths we each felt called to take. He admired initiative, and loved us far too much to impose his own will on us.

What the nuns taught us, more than anything academic, was how to live, how to love and how to pray. We saw what dedication meant – we weren't told about it, we saw it, in them. We saw what it was to love God so much that the joy of that love overflowed all bounds, and gave vitality and strength in even the most demanding situations. And we learnt, or rather began to learn, about prayer. We had always prayed, first of all saying the little prayers that Mother taught us when we were small, then progressing to a kind of ease of conversation with God and with our favourite saints. But seeing the sisters kneeling or sitting in the chapel in silent adoration before God made a new and very deep impression on us. We knew they were human, so full of fun, sometimes so quick to correct us, and yet during their times of prayer we saw them mute in the presence of the One they loved passionately. Perhaps they too were still learning to pray, as I've been trying to learn for the past fifty years and more, and no doubt I'll always be a learner; but prayer is one of those things in life where even the smallest experience brings untold blessings. One of the good things about being a learner is having a teacher; and when the teacher is God (though He often uses intermediaries) one can be sublimely confident of the outcome; and the rest does not matter very much.

I took to slipping into the Convent chapel to pray when I had some free time, and to going to Mass every day. There were no rules about Mass-going, because a lot of the boarders were not Catholics; but we could go if we felt so inclined.

I loved going – I hope it was for the Lord, though as with most things my motives were mixed, and part of me liked to be seen to go. I don't suppose that God minded very much either way. As time went on I realised more and more that this was the environment where I belonged; and the thought of becoming a Carmelite nun, which had lain like a dormant seed in the depths of my consciousness all those years, was reawakened.

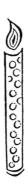

chapter thirteen

A big decision

At length the long, hard winter gave way to soft spring days, and Glastonbury and its environs were clothed in their blossom-decked greenness again after the muddy snow of so many weeks. Tennyson has the *Island Valley of Avilion* (Glastonbury) looking like this all the time – 'where falls not rain or hail, nor any snow'. We felt he hadn't lived there, or at any rate not long enough, though we loved the poem. We had our first experience of Holy Week services and thought them wonderful, as we have both done every year since. Then, as the summer came on, so did exams. Those of us who were to take them went to Wells, to the Blue School, which was the nearest centre. Wells has ever since been very close to my heart – we had the opportunity of exploring it, in between the exams. We went into the cathedral, or sat by the moat watching the swans. If it happened that I was on my own - for we were taking different subjects from one another – I would go into the chapel of the Carmelite monastery which was there in those days, and spend some time in prayer. I was also hoping that I would hear the nuns chanting. I looked at the big black grille at the side of the sanctuary, and wondered what life would be like behind it.

Before the term ended I actually went to visit the Carmelites, and plucked up the courage to tell them I was thinking of entering Carmel myself. They thought I was still very young, though by then I had turned eighteen. They told me to learn all I could before entering. I thought they must mean things that used the mind, and set myself to work harder at my Latin; but of course they meant practical skills like plumbing, gardening and mending fuses.

However, as things turned out, I was not to become a nun yet. My year at school finished, I returned home, and carried on with my study and with living a normal life there as before – only now we had Julian, who was by then six months old and full of life. He had been born on Boxing Day, while we were at home for the Christmas holidays. His birthday added yet another dimension to those beautiful days. Mother wasn't well for some time after his arrival. I think she had put all her strength into having this wonderful, bonny little son, and was run-down for a year or so afterwards. She suffered from muscular rheumatism in her knees, which made life difficult for her. So she was glad to have me at home to help, and I soon became another mother to Julian, doing everything for him and loving every minute.

Bou had to go back to school alone the next term, so for the first time in our lives we were separated. To begin with, she tried coming home for a few hours on occasional Sundays, just to be with us all; but I felt she wasn't very happy there on her own. She was in some ways very different from me, even though we had so much in common; and she was more observant, and very sensitive towards other people. I think she used to get anxious about how we all were at home. After a while she transferred to another school run by the same sisters – the Sisters of Charity of St Louis – at Minehead; and she stayed there for over a year until she, too, was eighteen.

Meanwhile I had written to the Carmelite monastery at Exmouth, in Devon, to ask if they would receive me as a possible candidate, as the monastery at Wells was not able to take any more recruits just then. They asked me to come and visit them, which I did, and thereafter I kept in contact by letter. The Prioress used to send me books to read. In those days you could send books by post very cheaply as long as they didn't contain a letter – a special book rate. I wanted to enter Carmel, yet felt I was needed at home – in fact, I was torn by many conflicting emotions at that time. I wanted to earn some money, to try to repay a little of what I felt I owed to the family; wanted to help at home; and wanted to go to Carmel. Mainly I was getting cold feet about Carmel, but I didn't see that at the time – or didn't want to. Yet God used this delay and it was all part of his plan for me, because I learned a lot during this time that was to stand me in good stead in years to come; I would have been very immature if I had entered earlier, and had to have much of the stuffing knocked out of me later on.

98

As it was, a good bit of spadework was done while I was still at home! Even though, after all these years, there is still plenty left to do.

Simon, too, had gone away to boarding school during that time, with the Christian Brothers. He was eleven, a growing boy of woods and fields, very sensitive and shy. It must have been a traumatic experience for him, far more than any of us realised at the time. We thought his dread of going back after the holidays was just the normal school-boy reaction, but it really went much deeper and he suffered considerably. He was very bright and, though he hadn't bothered much about his lessons at home, he was always top or second of his class at school. Bridget missed him dreadfully. She was three years younger than he, but they were great pals, and she was always with him and his friends in all their escapades. It was a case of tolerating a girl in their group because of her usefulness – she was often (though not always!) willing to do the fetching and carrying and other chores for them.

The following September she also went to school. She was eight, and went as a weekly boarder, a situation which Bou and I felt was not entirely satisfactory. The boarders would be together over the weekend, and the group would close in, as it were, leaving any who went home for those days on the outside. By Friday they would have become part of the group again, only to leave that evening and break the close relationship anew. But it did mean she was with the family, so I suppose both sides have to be weighed. We always tried to have a baked potato sitting in the oven of the kitchen range ready for her return on Friday evenings; she loved baked potatoes, and didn't get them at school. Once she was sitting down with her potato she knew she was home. The double kind of existence must have been a strain for a little girl. After I had left home, when she was twelve, she also transferred to the Minehead school as a full-time boarder.

As the Convent was next door to the church, Bou and I continued to call in to see the Sisters after we had been to Mass on Sundays. Those were the days before the relaxing of the long fast before going to Communion, so we were glad to avail ourselves of the cup of tea kindly offered us. Coffee and refreshments for the congregation after church services were unheard of in those days, in England at any rate. On one such morning Sister Patricia, who was at that time headmistress, asked me if I would consider coming to the school in the afternoons to help out with the teaching, as they were having difficulties and needed help. It sounded like a *cri de coeur,* so after giving the matter some thought I said I would. The pay she offered was very low, even for those days, and I don't think the Sisters realised I'd have to spend part of it on my bus fare. But it was money, and I knew they hadn't much of it themselves.

So I became a teacher, first just for the afternoons, and then full-time. I was now working with the nuns as a colleague instead of a pupil, and got to know them on a different level. I was even more amazed at what Sister Eugenie managed to do in a day – yet she always appeared to have plenty of time for everyone. Not only the children who came to the school, but their mothers, grannies, other relatives, people who came to church – she knew all their problems and needs and they all felt that she loved them and cared about them. As well as being compassionate towards other people's sufferings she was also very sensitive herself, as I now realised, and often suffered deeply from the clashes and bashes of daily living in a busy school.

Teaching was rather fun, once I had got over the initial shyness of hearing my own voice in a fairly hushed classroom. Many of the girls had been pupils with me a couple of years before. Sometimes I had the little ones, which was a challenging experience but one which I loved; I was used to caring for tiny tots. We nearly always seemed to have a few toddling around in our house, not only our own but other people's as well, for my parents liked to feel the house was open to them all. Occasionally I took the next class, who were a real problem, neither small enough to behave nor old enough for any serious work. I always found myself counting the minutes when I was in that class, though their own regular teacher thought them wonderful. I think they saw me coming, and knew what they could get away with. Outside of class they were as lovely as all the other children, with their shining eyes and eager questions. Probably they were just too young to be expected to sit in a classroom for two hours at a stretch – it was no longer the 'playing' class of the kindergarten.

After a few terms, Sister Patricia was moved to the nuns' school at Frome. She took me with her to help, and I became a weekly boarder there. Again it was quite a small school in terms of numbers, under a hundred all told, so with the five classes there were less than twenty children in each. I had my own form there, though I had sessions with some of the other classes when mine were otherwise engaged. Mine were the older girls, some not much younger than I was – just a small group, but we got on well together. One of them entered with the Sisters not long after I came to Carmel, and did great work, first in the school and later in their nursing home at Minehead. Sadly, she died of cancer when only in her fifties.

Frome (pronounced *Froom*) is a charming little town, parts of it very old indeed. It had been a wool town in days gone by. Some of the streets had fascinating names – there was Milk Street and Wine Street; and Gentle Street (or was it Cheap Street?) had a little channel of rushing water running down the centre. Catherine Hill and Catherine Street owed their names to the days when the Dominicans had had a Friary there, or nearby.

There were two other lay-teachers also living in, so I made new friends as well as getting to know another community of nuns. In the summer evenings the three of us sometimes went for a walk, and explored the beautiful surrounding countryside. On winter evenings we prepared lessons, and I did knitting and needlework. The other two went out, now and again, to films or dances; but my money was too precious. In any case, I was glad of the chance to have time to be quiet and spend in prayer or reading. I found the work very demanding, and realised that, if ever I became a permanent teacher, I'd need some training in channelling the high spirits of the young!

Again, the school buildings had been built onto an existing 'gentleman's residence'; but it was much longer established than the Glastonbury school, and I found the long, dark corridors quite spooky. My room was in the main house, up on the second floor, which was very high because the rooms in those old, grander

101

houses had high ceilings. Yet the japonica bush that grew beside the front door, and covered almost all the front of the house, reached right up to my window. That japonica is my special 'flower memory' of the Frome days, though there were many other lovely flowers there as well, both in the garden and beyond.

On Friday evenings I went home, my weekly wage tucked, oh so carefully, in my pocket, and any other bits and pieces I had been able to collect to take home stuffed into my little case. Sometimes the sisters gave me things to take for the family, such as some fruit. I managed to save a bit of my butter ration some weeks – rationing still kept everything on short rein, and any foodstuffs were eagerly accepted. On the Saturday morning I felt so proud to be able to produce a pound note – well over half of my pay – for Mother to take to the shop for the weekly grocery order. It paid for it all – not the bread, meat or milk which were bought elsewhere, but all the rest – and a few biscuits for the youngest member of the family.

I loved the time at Frome, and met lots of interesting people. My reading habits had changed a good deal by now, and I read eagerly the religious books lent to me by the Prioress at Exmouth Carmel, and any others I could lay my hands on. I had at last begun to do what Father had always advocated when reading – to 'read, mark, learn and inwardly digest' a book, rather than avidly read through straight off. He used to say to us, when we finished off our new Christmas book on Boxing Night, that we couldn't possibly have read it properly in so short a time! The books I now read were the kind you could begin again once you reached the last page, and find more and more to savour. But, though there was so much to see, and to do and to enjoy, my thoughts turned more and more towards Carmel.

When the time came to return home for the summer holidays, I told Sister Patricia that I should not be coming back next term. I found it hard to talk about entering Carmel – I was always very shy in any case, and anything so personal and likely to be misunderstood I kept closely to myself. Yet I felt I should give my reason for wanting to leave Frome, especially as I had been so happy there. Fortunately she did understand and was very kind though I had the feeling she would have preferred me to join the sisters there. She said she would be glad to have me back at the school, if I found that Carmel was not my vocation.

It was hard to leave those sisters, and all my other friends there. But the summer holidays beckoned, and I wanted those last precious days with my family. A letter from the Prioress at Exmouth had just arrived, in which I felt that even her Job-like patience might be running on the lees. She suggested that one can live a life of prayer and closeness to God 'in the world' just as well as in Carmel – in other words, maybe that was what I should be doing, since I seemed in no hurry to enter. It was the prod I needed. I realised she probably would not have known all my reasons and inner aches, why I had appeared to drag my feet, or my apparent lack of commitment. I knew perfectly well that I could never be completely happy until I had tried to be a Carmelite. I was by now, if the truth be told, too much in love with God to be able to wait much longer anyway.

That holiday, my last at home, though outwardly sunny and happy, was fraught with anguish for me. I had given the Prioress at Exmouth a date when I should arrive, and yet I couldn't for the life of me tell them all at home. Somehow I couldn't even tell Bou, though we were so very close. In fact, often we didn't talk about very personal things with one another – we somehow knew without words how the other felt. The days crept by – no, they flew. 'I'll say it tomorrow', I kept telling myself, thinking or rather hoping that a suitable opportunity would arrive. August passed, a friend came to stay, then she went home. 'I'll tell them when she's gone', I thought. But no. I just couldn't bear to do it. I wasn't brave enough. I felt they wouldn't be able to bear it – they could surely not survive seeing me going down the road, knowing that I would never come home again. But I had to say something — for a start, I would have to ask Father for the train-fare to Exmouth, because I had no money left of my own. Every morning I got up planning that this would be the day. But things happened, other events crowded in, and by bed-time I was no further forward. It was awful.

September came, and Simon and Bridget went back to school. I suddenly had the bright idea that I would distemper my bedroom,

103

and leave it looking smart after I had gone. So I bought a tin of cheap bright pink emulsion paint. Just at that very time, Bridget was sent home with mumps. She shared the room with me, because she had a tendency to sleep-walk, and needed to be with someone strong enough to help her back into bed if this happened; the stairs in that house would have been very dangerous for anyone not in control, had she walked that far. 'Bother', I thought, 'just as I was going to paint the room'. But, foolish as I was, I covered Bridget's bed, patient and all, with newspaper, and carried on doggedly with distempering the walls. Mother was horrified, and said that at my age I ought to have known better – 'Bridget with a temperature, too, surrounded by those damp walls'. But the patient herself didn't seem to be at all concerned; she thought it all rather fun – much better than being in bed feeling poorly all on her own.

It would have helped the situation if some or at least one of my friends had also decided to enter a convent or monastery. But though none of us was aware of it at the time, the downward trend in the number of people entering religious orders had already begun. It was to escalate dramatically over the next three decades. At that time every town, even every small town, had a convent, some more than one. Most ran a school, some a hospital or nursing home, and there were always the contemplative houses like the Carmelites who devoted their lives to prayer and praise. All the towns near home – Glastonbury, Bridgwater, Taunton, Wells, Shepton Mallet, Burnham-on-Sea – each had its convent. Today they have all gone. The religious orders and institutes to which they belonged have in most cases flourishing houses abroad; but Europe and the United States have suffered a great slump in religious vocations. However, there is still great dedication, especially among the young, and many new movements are springing up that are most praiseworthy in their service of people in need. In the southern hemisphere vocations abound.

Incredibly, as it seems to me now, the day of my departure dawned and I still hadn't told them.

chapter fourteen

To Carmel at Exmouth

That morning I was downstairs quite early, soon after Father had come down the creaky stair and put the kettle on for his customary task of making the early morning tea.

'I'm just going to pop down to Exmouth to see Mother Prioress for a few days', I said breezily. 'Have you any money I could have for the fare?' He patted his empty trouser pocket. 'I haven't a bean, my duck', he answered truthfully. 'My duck' was his term of endearment, and whenever he was quite broke – which was nearly all the time – he referred to it as 'not having a bean'. So I knew it was true. My heart sank even lower, and he must have observed its position somehow. So he came up with an idea. I was to go to Street, which cost fourpence on the bus (I had that much myself). There, I was to go into the bank, and see if he had anything left in his account. If he had, bring it, he said, and he and Mother would be at the bus stop as my bus returned through the village. If I got off, that would mean that there wasn't a bean in the bank either and we'd all walk back up the road and home. If I 'struck oil' – another of his phrases – I could go on to Exmouth and he and Mother would go to Bridgwater for the morning.

So I took an old canvas shopping bag that I thought no one would miss – there were no plastic carriers in those days – hurried upstairs, and put my few belongings into it. Wearing my hat and coat, I put my head round the door of Mother's bedroom, where she was still in bed sipping her tea.

'I'm just going down to see Mother Prioress', I said, very fast. I had been once before and had come safely home; and I hoped I'd sound so casual that this would appear to be simply a repeat performance. I must have succeeded – though whether they really guessed all the time I'll never know. I persuaded myself that I wasn't actually telling them a lie – after all, I *would* be seeing Mother Prioress. In my heart I knew it was an elopement – yet

105

even there I was still so unsure of myself and my ability to persevere in my resolve.

Then I hurried off down the lane to the bus-stop, feeling dreadful but knowing that I must go on, having got this far. Street was only about three miles away – we often walked there, when there was time. To my relief, the bank handed me some cash in response to the note Father had given me to take. It wasn't time yet for the return bus to Ashcott, so I got on one for Glastonbury, a couple of miles further on. I looked from the bus window at the Tor – our Tor, so much a part of our lives – and tried to say goodbye to it.

Once I reached Glastonbury, I ran like a demented creature down to the Convent and into the nearest classroom, which was the kindergarten. I whispered briefly to the sister who was teaching, saying where I was going and begging her prayers. Then off I fled, just in time to catch the bus that returned through Ashcott and on to Bridgwater.

There at Ashcott bus stop stood my parents and Julian, expectantly watching to see whether I would get off to join them, or wait for them to join me. I beckoned them in, and handed the money from the bank to Father, apart from the cost of my ticket to Exmouth. The bus pulled its way up the steep hill through the village, and I looked at the familiar houses as they slipped past – the big cedar tree, the walnut tree, the Post Office – I would almost certainly never see them again. Surely my parents must have seen my face – yet maybe they suspected nothing.

It was a pretty journey, through the Somerset country villages, and one that we always enjoyed; but for me on that day it all seemed to rush past in a blur, though it was a sunny October day. When we reached Bridgwater we all got off at the nearest stop to the station, and we parted. I went down the road towards the station, and the other three up towards the town and the river. It was a long, straight road, and after a few moments I turned and looked back at them. My parents were walking and maybe talking – oh, how dear they were to me, as I looked at their backs getting further and further away! And there was little Julian, holding on to Mother's hand but walking backwards, waving his free hand at me. I waved and waved until they were out of sight. He was only four years old. I was not to see him again for almost twenty years, when he was a Cambridge graduate and well over six feet tall, but still the same dear brother.

Bridgwater station seemed quite big to me then, though, as now, there was only one line each way; however, it was the main line to the west, and fairly busy. I was unused to rail travel, though I had been to Exeter a couple of times before with Father. He used to have to go there now and again to have a new fitting for the leather support-case he sometimes wore on what remained of his right arm.

At Exeter station I had to disembark and go to another station across the city for the smaller country train down to Exmouth. I had taken a return ticket, knowing that I hadn't enough money to buy two singles and fearing that I might be sent away from Carmel and need to get home. It just didn't occur to me that the nuns would give me my fare and any other money I needed, should the situation arise!

Soon there it was: Exmouth station, and I had to find my way to the Carmel. It was not far, and before long I was ringing the doorbell. In those days the extern sisters, who looked after the visitors and did the shopping, etc, had a little cottage adjoining the main house, where they lived together and cared for the chapel and the visitors' rooms and garden. I stayed in their cottage for the first night, and they kindly suggested that I might like to go for a walk on my last morning 'outside', to see the sea for the last (and in the case of Exmouth beach, the first) time. So I walked down the town, and onto the sea-shore, and saw the gulls and other sea-birds wheeling above the water and the sand. It was a cool autumnal morning, and there were few people about; I had the beach almost to myself. I walked a little, then lay down on the sand, in my smart tweed coat and all, in sheer agony of heart and mind. I knew I wanted Carmel so much, and felt that it was where God was calling me; yet I was already desperately homesick.

I must have lain there quite some time; but I was calmer when I got up, and started to walk back, looking around at the beautiful scenery. I began to be more practical in thought, and reasoned that everyone has to leave home at some stage and that I would have had to do it anyway. Also, it might turn out that I was not a suitable candidate for the life of Carmel. If that happens, I decided, I would see if the sisters at the convent at Glastonbury would like me to join them. And if they, too, found me unsuitable, I would buy a lovely blue plaid dress, such as I had just seen in a shop window – an autumn dress, made of warm material, but very attractive. I fancied it no end. It looked just like 'me'.

Then it was back to Carmel where at 2 p.m. I was to enter. The extern sisters took me to the big enclosure door, which was unbolted from within and slowly drawn open. Inside, in the cloister, there were several nuns, with veils pulled right over their faces, to welcome me. The Prioress had her veil turned back, so I knew her at once. When the big door had been closed and bolted again, the others turned back their veils and I saw smiling, welcoming faces, to my relief. The Prioress took my hand and led me up the cloister and into the choir, which was the sisters' part of the chapel. Together we knelt for a few moments, to say a silent prayer. I was in Carmel at last.

The Prioress then took me upstairs to my cell, as our bedrooms are called in Carmel. They are not just for sleeping in but also the sisters spend time in them, reading, praying and sometimes working. It is the little private place that each one has, where she can be alone in silence. I loved mine the moment I saw it – it was just as I had seen in pictures of Carmelite cells in books – very simple, with cream-washed walls, a bed alongside the wall covered with a brown serge blanket, a little stool and a window seat. There was a large window for the size of the room, and it had wooden shutters. There were no curtains, carpets, or cushions anywhere in the house; the benches and stools were of cheap but well-kept wood. The cells measured ten feet by eight feet (three metres by two and a half). The bed felt incredibly hard. I couldn't think what it could be made of. Later I discovered it was a tightly-packed straw palliasse, extremely heavy, laid on three planks. All the beds were the same. I was glad that there were plenty of blankets, and was in fact told to be sure to ask for more if I needed them. I was a chilly mortal, and knew how cold a convent can be in midwinter.

I looked out of my window, and saw that it faced East, and would get the early morning sunshine. It looked out across the laundry roof to the garden beyond, where I saw fruit trees, and a well-arranged vegetable garden. There was a grassy walk, and a patch of flowers against the walls. It's not going to be so bad, after all, I thought.

The Prioress at that time was a remarkable lady, kind, strong, much loved and considered by all who knew her to be very holy. She seemed very old to me, at twenty-two, but she was actually about 69 or 70, which I now think of as being late middle-aged. She came from an ancient Catholic family, the Vavasours, and had grown up at Hazlewood Castle in Yorkshire, which had been the family's ancestral home since the time of the Norman conquest. Hers was the last generation to grow up there. Like so many of those huge old houses and castles, it became impossible for a family to maintain and she had the sadness of seeing it sold. Later it came back into Catholic hands when the Carmelite Friars took it on as a Retreat and Conference Centre, and this was still going well at the time of her death, when she was in her nineties. Since then, the friars have also found the beautiful but large and uneconomical building too expensive to run, and they have quite recently had to sell it, much to their own and many other people's sadness.

Mother Mary of St John, as she was called in Carmel, had entered the Carmel at Notting Hill in London in her twenties. At that time numerous Carmels were being founded all over England, Scotland and Wales. It was a time of expansion and of many vocations. Not long after completing her Novitiate, she was sent to one of the new foundations. Her gifts were quickly recognised, and while still young she found herself appointed Prioress of a new Carmel. She had great charm as well as a good head for business. She was also a woman of prayer and able to imbue others with her own high ideals; yet at the same time she had a winning simplicity, and could enjoy the small things in life and the funny incidents that crop up so often, yet are lost on many people. She must have found life in Carmel very different from her previous life of London high society and a castle full of servants for her home. I only began to realise that as the months went by.

109

She had been sent to Exmouth as its founding Prioress in 1926, just twenty-five years before I entered there, and had been at the helm ever since. She was to remain in office until 1960 and even after that she was very much part of the community's governing body. I was fortunate in having such a wise and kindly Prioress. She could be very firm – something I had never had to experience in my life before; but she was never harsh. It was part of the training in those days to bring up the young ones to take correction – not just in Carmel but in all walks of life. Any young person doing an apprenticeship in a craft or job was 'treated tough'.

After depositing my pathetic little bag of belongings in my cell I was left to look around on my own, so I had a peep at part of the garden. I loved the trees – I felt that they were friends I knew, whereas everyone in the house was a stranger. I also saw flowers and bushes that I recognised, and others that were new to me; and I began to get my bearings.

I met the whole Community at the evening recreation for the first time, when we all sat round in the community room. All except the very old sat on the floor, as the custom was at the time. The habits were made of thick material, and could be tucked under one's feet and ankles so that it was quite a comfortable position to be in. We always sat like that during our times of prayer, and also if we were sewing or doing other handiwork, or writing in our cells. They sat around that evening, in their brown habits and black veils. There were two novices who wore the customary white veils of those who are not yet finally committed to stay for the rest of their lives in Carmel. The Prioress told me their names but I couldn't remember them all at once – there were fourteen sisters there. There were also three extern sisters, who didn't come into the enclosure for recreation (or anything else unless some work was needed that only they could do) but they were considered to be, and were, very much part of the Community.

At last it was time for bed, and I went thankfully up to my little cell. I cried into the pillow for a long time before I went to sleep. I've done it now, I thought. Yet deep down I was glad. As far as I could see then, and indeed as I see it still, I had done the best I could. Only those who have lived through this experience can have

110

any idea what it is like.

At half-past five next morning I heard the clapper that signalled it was time for all the sisters to rise. I had been told not to stir until someone knocked on my door. So I lay and listened, as little movements in the cell next to mine indicated that my neighbour was getting up. Soon I heard soft footsteps as the rope-soled alpargates passed my door on the way down to the choir. Then all was silent again. I knew they had all gone down to sing Lauds, the first prayer of the day, a great expression of praise. I felt lonely surrounded by empty cells. It was still quite dark.

After about half an hour the sister who had been detailed to keep an eye on me and help me find my way around knocked on my door. She came in, bringing with her a long black dress, a little black cape that reached to the elbows, and a black net cap that tied under the chin with a bow of black satin ribbon. How awful! I thought. These were to be my clothes for the first six months of my life in the monastery as a postulant, or new-comer. Nowadays postulants wear their own clothes, but this was 1951 and things were still more or less as they had been for the last few hundred years.

At that time, too, when a girl became a nun, part of the complete change-over to the new life was the taking of a new name. I was given the name of Sister Elizabeth. Thank God, it's not one of those extraordinary names I've read about in books about nuns, thought I. It was a beautiful name, and I was happy with it. But seeing myself in this curious black get-up, and being called Sister or Sister Elizabeth took some getting used to. I was glad none of the family ever came to see me during those six months – I shouldn't have wanted them to see me looking like that!

Once I was rigged out in these sombre clothes, my own things were taken upstairs to a cupboard near the Novitiate. Then it was time for Mass. I felt I was on my own ground there, because Mass is the same everywhere and I had for years attended it whenever I had the chance. It was all in Latin but I was deeply and lovingly familiar with it. I felt renewed and refreshed.

After Mass we all went to the refectory, which is the monastic name for the dining-room. There we had a very simple breakfast

– in those days it was taken standing – and then everyone went off to her appointed work in the house or garden. Breakfast was a chunk of bread and a bowl of hot water with sugar in it. For the first few days I found the latter revolting, but as the winter came on I was only too glad to get it and became accustomed to this unusual beverage. I'm glad to say this kind of breakfast has now been superseded, but it is still a very simple repast.

I was given various tasks to do, as the days went on. They all seemed very dull and uninteresting. I had been accustomed to a degree of responsibility in the school and at home, and felt I was just being given jobs to keep me occupied. In one way I suppose this was indeed so. For those first days and weeks I needed to learn how to do the work, and where things were, and that meant someone had to take the time to instruct me. Everyone had her own schedule to fulfil, and little time to spare. I swept the choir, and did an hour's gardening – this was more up my street – and sewed, and helped make altar-breads. Gradually I learned what to do – and what not to do! Then there were the times set aside for prayer. I was happy then – they were the best parts of the day.

We also had a little free time, when we could go for a walk in the garden, or have a rest, or write our letters. It was a well-balanced life, with work and rest, prayer and recreation alternating throughout the day, never too long of one thing at a stretch. At first I found the silence quite hard to get accustomed to. The house was kept very quiet – no one clattered about, or talked in the passages. Talking was kept to a minimum, except during the periods of recreation. I remember thinking how I'd like to start at the top of the house and come all the way down making the most tremendous noise. I'd always lived among children, with their voices and often their shrieks, and howls, and laughter making background music to whatever I was doing. At home we often sang as we worked, too, though we were never a family for leaving the radio on, even when we had one. As the days went by, I began to appreciate the silence and realise how valuable a setting it created for the practice of prayer – in fact, its indispensability for the kind of life that Carmelites live.

The main reason for my finding both the work and the silence difficult in those first few days was that I was in a sense still suffering from the bereavement of leaving so closely-knit a family. I felt as if I'd had several limbs amputated, and all my teeth out. One day I was told I was going to learn how to bake the altar-breads. I duly went along to the room where this work was done – on gas-rings in those days. Nowadays large electric machinery is used which eliminates a lot of work and expenditure of time and energy. I was shown how to ladle the flour and water paste onto the hot, shiny surface of the metal plates, which were then clamped together tightly so that the residue of the paste squeezed out at the sides, hissing and spluttering. Once it had gone quiet the sheet of wafer inside was cooked, and one opened up the clamp and removed the smooth, white wafer from the plate, laid it aside and put another ladle in. I was a bit scared of gas – we had nothing of that kind at home. Also the hissing and sizzling was somewhat disconcerting; but I carried on for a while. A little later the sister who had initiated me into this new art returned to see how I was getting on. My sheets of wafer were sitting there on the table – not the supple, smooth white ones such as the previous baker had produced, but dull, and cracked, and yellow coloured. Sister Teresa looked at them thoughtfully. 'Did you give a good rub to the plates with that oily cloth each time?' she asked. She'd actually told me to do that. 'No', I replied. 'Why ever not?' she asked, kindly, but clearly puzzled. 'Oh, I couldn't be bothered!' I answered cheerfully. In the world from which I had come, not being able to be bothered was a perfectly legitimate excuse for not having done something.

But this was Carmel, and the livelihood of the Community depended to a great extent on the production of these altar-breads. Sister Teresa was a lovely, great-hearted, kind person whom I soon grew to admire and love a lot. 'Well', she said without any fluster, 'you'll have to learn to be bothered'. So that was the simple but profound way I learned the next big lesson. In many ways I am still trying to learn it.

113

Glastonbury Tor

The family home in Ashcott

chapter fifteen

A way of giving

The Community to which I had come ranged in age from Sister Catherine, who was two years older than me, to Sister Anne, well into her eighties. This seems to be the pattern in most Carmels. Because it is a fairly rare calling, people enter one at a time, with maybe several years between. Also, they come at any age between twenty and occasionally even over fifty, so we usually have one or two in each decade of their lives. This is healthy, because it means that the interplay between young, middle-aged, and older sisters helps to stretch the capacity of each to accept and learn from the others.

Maybe I should say a little here about how it all began – about the origins of the Carmelite Order. As its name implies, it started on Mount Carmel, in Israel. The earliest documentation available dates the giving of a Rule of Life to a group of hermits living there early in the thirteeth century. For how many years, centuries even, hermits had been there before that is not known; but, when Christianity returned for a time to Jerusalem and the surrounding area towards the end of the eleventh century, it is probable that Mount Carmel soon became a treasured abode of men who sought a life of prayer and solitude, alone with God in the hidden places of the rocks. They looked back to the prophet Elijah, who had lived and prayed on this mountain, and found the Lord not in the fire nor in the whirlwind but in the whisper of a gentle breeze. Carmelites down the ages since have found inspiration in this mysterious encounter with the unseeable God. They have sought the divine mystery in prayer and solitude, and there taken part in the struggle between good and evil at the heart of the world's conflicts.

At the time of the Crusades, when the Saracens were besieging the holy places, the brothers of Mount Carmel were driven from their dwellings and scattered far and wide. The first small group to arrive in England was brought here by knights returning from a Crusade in 1242. Houses also began to spring up all over Europe, wherever the brothers could find lodgings, and the Order of Mount Carmel grew rapidly. By 1450 we begin to hear of houses for women. England by then had a large number of Carmelite friars.

It was in 1535 that the great St Teresa entered the Carmel of the Incarnation at Avila in Spain, by which time the way of life had changed and lost much of the original spirit of the Order. She lived there for about twenty years, until she felt that God was asking something more of her. After many tribulations and a great deal of heart-searching, Teresa left with a few companions to found St Joseph's, a new small monastery in which she planned and hoped that the original Rule of Carmel would be kept. In the very large community at the Incarnation this had not been possible. Teresa has left us the account of the founding of St Joseph's in her own sparkling, energetic words. There was a great deal of opposition to the new Carmel, and it was some time before she herself was able to live there in peace. Eventually the hostility died down, and Teresa was asked to found more of these houses of prayer in other cities of Spain. She introduced a fresh orientation into Carmelite life, combining silence and solitude with community living and giving us the specific mission of praying for the Church and for all the peoples of the world.

Today St Teresa is looked upon as the great inspirer of our Carmels. Her books are still being read and reprinted after four hundred years. Since her time there have been other well known Carmelites, particularly St Thérèse of Lisieux at the end of the last century and Sister Elizabeth of Dijon at the beginning of this. A notable figure of our own era is Edith Stein, a Jewish philosopher who entered Carmel after becoming a Catholic and eventually died in the gas chambers of Auschwitz under the Nazi regime.

Carmelites are not a special kind of people, as you will by now have realised, but very ordinary women, drawn from many walks of life, who at some point have felt the need to give themselves entirely to serving the Lord in prayer. For some the decision comes quickly as a certainty, for others it emerges as a gradual process in a long search for God's will.

Once made, the decision is not binding until a trial period of about five years has passed, a time for exploring the meaning of the Carmelite life and how it is lived out in daily commitment. At first, there is the different life-style to get accustomed to – the house is simply furnished with just the essentials, the food is rather plain but adequate and wholesome. The atmosphere is silent, though it is a silence which conveys love, joy and peace within the community. Daily life is structured around the Mass and the official prayer of the Church, the Divine Office.

All of this I found out gradually, as the days passed; and I realised that I was only one in an immensely long tradition. Over the centuries countless numbers of people have been drawn into a deep, personal, intimate relationship with God; and this continues into our own time. In fact, more and more people today feel the need of stepping aside for a while from the rush of daily living. 'Come aside to a lonely place'.

For some people this need to step into silence, into a desert place, becomes more of a demand. As they begin to pray more, to cherish moments of stillness with God more deeply, and to understand something of what prayer can bring about, they feel the call to devote themselves totally to it. A new apostolate opens out to them, and prayer becomes an attractive and powerful means of serving the Church and all mankind.

The call to seek God is a call rising from the well-springs of the human heart, which is always longing for something, someone beyond itself. This same searching and striving lies behind all the greatest achievements of men and women down the ages. It drove the explorers to push their way through immeasurable hardships in order to go further into the mysterious unknown, where they sought to discover the beyond. It drives people today to go to the moon, and to want to go further still; it causes scientists to delve unremittingly into the hidden potential of living organisms.

St Augustine put it all very simply when he said that we shall go on longing and desiring and seeking until we reach God himself, because our whole being is created for Him, and ultimately we cannot be satisfied with anyone or anything less. It was this longing deep within me that had brought me to Carmel, inspired by reading the life of St Thérèse for the first time so many, many years before, and often since. She had become a Carmelite nun in answer to that call, and found in the monastery what she called her 'Little Way' to God. I wanted to follow that way.

In the early days of Christianity there were some who sold all they had and went to live in the desert, to spend all their lives in prayer and praise of God who is Love and who is supremely to be loved. This vocation has gone on throughout the history of the Church. The contemplative houses of today, though no longer usually situated in an actual desert, carry on the tradition of being places set apart. They provide both the desert atmosphere, where there is nothing to draw away the searching heart from its pursuit of God, and at the same time an oasis wherein to quench its unceasing thirst.

The Teresian Carmel is within this hermit tradition, though combined with a community life, fostering the spirit of the first Christian community 'united in heart and soul and sharing all things in common'. There are over 850 monasteries of Carmelite nuns today, scattered in all continents, where the sisters 'watch and pray'. In prayer they gather together the whole world's needs and sorrows, confident that Jesus meant what he said when he told his disciples, 'Ask and you shall receive'.

Their enclosed way of life is no separation from the pressing concerns of humanity. The cries of the poor and the powerless, expressed so poignantly in the psalms of the Divine Office, are in the hearts of the sisters constantly, as well as on their lips when they participate day after day in Carmel's monastic liturgy.

However urgent the needs of the active apostolate, there's no doubt that there will always be a place in the Church for people who are willing and happy to devote their lives to this hidden work of prayer, witnessing to the immediacy and supremacy of God's presence – 'looking to the Lord' in praise and worship, and interceding for his people.

There were many moments during those first few weeks when I felt very far from being a witness to anyone or anything. I knew that I must sit down and write home to tell them all that I was going to stay in Carmel, at any rate unless I was sent away. In other words, I wouldn't be coming home. You cannot imagine the misery I went through, until the letter had been sent. I kept putting off writing it, but after about three weeks Mother Prioress told me firmly that it was far better for the family's sake that they should know the truth. I knew it, too, in my mind but it cost my heart so much. Eventually it was done, and sent off; but I knew it would cause so much pain, and I hated doing that. I had, of course, sent them a card when I had first arrived, to let them know I had had a safe journey and was being well looked after; but it had given no hint of the finality of the situation.

My parents must have felt it very much, because neither of them wrote to me for a very long time – they were unable to put into words what they felt, despite usually being such good letter-writers. As with the outbreak of war, and all the other trials they had shared, they carried on with living, and loving, and caring for their family. They had been brought up with the Edwardian attitude which held that it was neither desirable nor polite to show your feelings. What might in other circumstances have been a happy occasion – the fulfilment of a life's dream for their eldest daughter – was probably more of a bereavement. The sorrow lay in that it was hard for them to believe I should be really happy in Carmel. I had always been such a live-wire, and to them it must have looked as if I had been shut away forever in a very dull place. Bou bore the pain with the same silent courage and deep faith with which she has borne so much pain since; and all were upheld by the secret hope that one day, perhaps quite soon, I would come home.

What really kept me going during those early months and years in the monastery was Bou's letters. She was the one who kept me fully abreast of all that was happening at home – she wrote for them all. She told me all the little homely details she knew I would want to know, the funny incidents she was sure I would enjoy, also about what our friends were all doing. I blessed her for this loving labour. Years afterwards I used to tell people that – to use horticultural language – I hadn't been transplanted so much as layered. Bou's letters kept part of me anchored to home until I had really taken root in my new soil, and could fend for myself – or at

119

least not wilt away completely! In time she wrote less frequently, because she had very little time as her commitments increased; but to this day her beautifully crafted letters bring me much joy.

As the weeks went by I got to know the sisters, and the general pattern of the life. The garden was lovely, and I spent my bits of free time prowling around, looking at the plants and trees. There was a small wood at one side, fairly overgrown and wild, which was my special delight. One day, one of the sisters told me we were always free to sing while in the garden if we wished; no one would be disturbed by it out there. I had missed singing since I had been a nun – in the chapel everything in those days was sung in monotone – yes, *everything!* So I went off at the next opportunity and had a good sing among the trees in the little wood, or 'far garden' as we called it. Later that day, at recreation, I told the sister who had given me that good piece of information that I had done lots of singing, and had a lovely time. 'I'm so glad', she replied. 'It's nice to be able to sing all the hymns we used to know, isn't it?' Hymns! It had never occurred to me to sing hymns! The expression 'pop music' hadn't been coined then, but I had been singing its equivalent – all the tunes that everyone was singing or whistling at the time. I sang them to the Lord, indeed, as I always had, but I had never thought of classifying *The Chattanoogie Shoe-shine Boy* as a hymn!

Fortunately for me, having entered the Monastery in October meant that I only had to wait three months to Christmas. It was my first away from home, and very hard in a lot of ways; yet Christmas in Carmel – even in those days – is always so special, and it gave me a great boost. The strictness of the life is relaxed a bit and there is a real family spirit of celebration. To this day I look forward to Christmas with the eagerness of a child. I had been so lucky that I had learned during those home Christmasses what the meaning of it all was, and over the years the exploration of the mystery has only deepened my joy in the outward expression of the reality we commemorate.

In years to come I was much involved in the cookery side of the preparations for Christmas, but in those early days I was free to join in whatever was being organised. Several sisters would get up a play, or a concert or some other form of entertainment. Some met together and sang – there were several of us who had loved the Plain Chant in our churches before we entered, and we'd sing as much as we could remember without having the books.

At Christmas everyone could let their hair down, so to speak, at least in moderation! It was usually the newcomers who put up the crib, a task I loved doing. I think from that first Christmas to last I've always gone round the woods and garden on Christmas Eve, or maybe a day or two before, gathering the evergreens for the decorations. There is so much to bring in – berries, fungi, mossy bits of wood, cones, dried seed-pods, as well as the actual greenery. Not long ago we had a new young sister with us – it was her first Christmas in Carmel, and I felt for her, remembering how much it all means. She came out with me to gather the greenery and other decorations. She had grown up in a town, and had never seen berried holly growing on a tree. She thought it was always plastic. She was quite amazed at anyone going into garden and woods to get Christmas decorations – she had always bought man-made ones from the shops. I think she was quite intrigued with the way we did it here, though we do have tinsel as well. Although she didn't continue in Carmel, she appreciated her time spent with us. I like to think she still gets some of her Christmas décor from nature's bounty.

When the days of Christmas were over, it was back to work again, with Lent looming ahead like some kind of monster. I don't know why I thought Lent was going to be so hard – before I came to Carmel everyone gave something up for Lent, or did some extra good deed. I couldn't imagine what else we could give up! And so I suppose I expected it was going to be very penitential. I hadn't reckoned on the beauty and helpfulness of the Liturgy of those forty days, nor had I really grasped what it was all about. This came gradually, as the days unfolded before my eyes, in the breviary and the readings at Mass, the whole panorama of salvation history. I need not have been anxious. At the same time, spring was upon us, and the wintry garden blossomed into unspeakable beauty. Lent and spring-time are always inextricably intertwined in my vision, with the climax of both coming at Eastertide.

On one of the days early on in Lent I was called to the Prioress' office. This didn't happen often, so I wondered what it could mean. When I got there, having bounded up the stairs two at a time, she gave me the happy news that the Chapter of the monastery had given their vote for me to go ahead in the life, and I was to be given the Carmelite habit.

This is a big step forward in a nun's life. It means the end of postulancy (and in those days, of those black clothes!) and the beginning of the Novitiate proper. There would be more to learn, and more to take on board, but it was pointing in the right direction.

Today, the Clothing ceremony is a simple affair with only the community present. At that time it was a very solemn occasion, with lots of people attending, and usually a Bishop officiating – more as we would today celebrate the ceremony of taking Final Vows.

So the rest of Lent was a busy time, as the sisters concerned made my habit and veil, and the rope-soled shoes called alpargates which we all wore. Every now and again I had to have things tried on, and pinned, and re-measured – though really it seemed a bit of a waste of time to me, since the garments were all so voluminous when they were completed that I felt a few inches more or less wouldn't have made much difference!

Then there was the white dress. Those were the days when the girl receiving the Habit wore a bridal dress for the first part of the day and for the ceremony, then went out of the chapel at a certain moment to return in a few minutes wearing the basic Habit. The belt, scapular and veil were put on during the remainder of the service, each with its own significant blessing.

The monastery was poor in this world's goods, though rich, like my own home, in the things that matter most. Clothing ceremonies came round once in every few years. So the appropriate white bridal clothes were carefully packed away after use, against the next need. The result was that in the chest-of-drawers where they were kept there were several white (or by then decidedly off-white) garments of various dates over the twenty-five years of the foundation. I don't suppose that any had been bought by the monastery, but occasionally when a postulant had a sufficiently well-to-do family they would have bought something for her Clothing ceremony. Also, people sometimes gave their own wedding-dresses to convents and monasteries, either for a postulant to use on her Clothing day or to be used as material for making church vestments.

Wherever these had come from, the day I was taken into the infirmary where this chest-of-drawers stood, and was shown some of its treasures, I just stood there in a mixture of amusement, horror and hope. Sister Mary, who was the infirmarian and also looked after clothes for postulants, had told me that when the great morning came I would be attired in a lovely white bridal dress. I wasn't all that keen – I was very shy, and didn't fancy being dressed up conspicuously. 'It's brown I want, not white', I replied. But the white would come first, I was told, just for the first few hours. I wished I could have missed out that bit – future postulants are spared it. But I could see that for them it was part of the ceremony, and knew that I must go through with it with a good grace. So I set myself to enter into the spirit of it all, knowing that it would only last a short time, and the Habit, I sincerely hoped, would be mine (or its successors!) for the rest of my life.

Sister Mary pulled out a long, crumpled dress. 'I think this one's just your size', she said triumphantly. 'I'll give it a quick iron when you've tried it on'. Oh, dear – it was really *dreadful!* It had once been very pretty, no doubt, but it was a 1920s style, with a long bit hanging down at the back like part of a train; and it had seen better days. I dutifully tried it on.

'It's a bit tight', I said, trying to make myself look as fat as possible. I was really very vain, despite my outward scorn of fashion. I just could *not* be seen by my family in that dress.

To my great relief, the next she pulled out was much better – more modern and in good condition, pure white satin. I was deeply relieved. We then sorted through the white shoes; and we found a little net veil on a head-band. So now I was all set for my Clothing.

Carmelite Monastery at Exmouth

Thicket Priory

chapter sixteen

Novitiate

The week before the day of the Clothing was for me a special week of retreat. This was the custom, and it still is – a quiet week of prayer in preparation for the next big step in the new life. It was the end of April, and I sat in the garden a good deal. It was a happy time. Then on the evening before we had a quick run-through of the ceremony, so that I and everyone else knew what we all had to do and when to do it. The sisters were all so busy, gathering flowers for the chapel and making last minute preparations. My Habit was ready, hanging up in the robe room where it had been made; and the bridal dress hung in the infirmary. Then I thought about my hair. 'Help! Whatever could I do about that?' It had been tucked away under the black cap for all the six months of postulancy and had grown appreciably since I entered. I had always worn it fairly short, once my pigtails had been cut off – now it was an awkward length, straight as rats' tails – and in those days it just wasn't acceptable to have straight hair.

The sister who kept an eye on my needs came along after supper, to see if I had everything ready for the morrow. She'll help, I thought. I asked her if she could possibly get me some pieces of rag. She kindly obliged, though I think the request puzzled her somewhat. When she had gone, and I was undressed and ready for bed, I carefully rolled up bits of hair round the strips of rag as I used to at home in lieu of curlers. That's a problem solved, I said to myself, and went off to sleep.

Next morning I didn't want to take the 'curlers' out when I got up, for fear that my fragile curls would get flattened out under the black cap which I would have to wear at the beginning of the day. So I carefully put the cap on over the rags, which made my head a very knobbly shape, but I hoped no one would notice. The sisters are all very recollected – they'll never see, I thought. Wrong again! The first person to meet me was the Prioress, who greeted me warmly – it was my Clothing Day. Then she put her hand on my head in blessing. 'Whatever is this?' she exclaimed, feeling the knobs. 'It's curlers, Mother!' I said, with what I imagined was disarming enthusiasm. 'Take them out at once!' was her reply – though I did detect a twinkle in her eye. For years afterwards the sisters teased me about my curlers.

After Mass I was dressed up in all the white finery, and combed my curls into some semblance of a hair-do. Then, joy of joys, some of my family arrived. The kind priest from Glastonbury, knowing that they would not otherwise be able to be present for my special day, had offered to bring Bou, Simon and Bridget in his car, and also one of the Glastonbury sisters to represent the school there. It was wonderful to see them again. They hadn't brought Julian, because he was still too little to understand; and the day would have been too long for him. But the others were brimming over with excitement at seeing me again, and so was I. We had plenty of time for talking before lunch-time, and a bit afterwards. The ceremony was fixed for 2 p.m. Auntie Lucy and a friend had come by train, and a few of my other friends arrived as the day progressed. Sister Catherine's mother and sister came all the way from Manchester. They had recently been bereaved: Catherine's father had died very suddenly. They loved Carmel, and felt it would help to lift their sorrowing spirits to be present at a Clothing, especially as I was about Catherine's age, and was to be her close friend in the years that lay ahead. I loved having them there. My own mother and father had not been able to come, but having Catherine's mother gave that special mother-dimension to my day. One of the many lovely things about belonging to a small, closely-knit community is that we can share our relatives, in a sense. Actually many years later, long after my final vows, she confided to her daughter that at the time she thought that I was not likely to stay the course. Perhaps it was those curls!

Soon it was time for me to go to the chapel. Simon gave me away. He was fifteen, looking tall and smart in his dark suit, obligatory Sunday dress at his school. It was getting short in the sleeve and the pocket was darned (a mouse had tried to get to the sweets he had once left in it!) but I was so proud of him. Bridget had on a pretty pink dress that Bou had made, and a little veil that she had brought 'in case'. So she was my bridesmaid. As I went through the enclosure door I turned and gave the three of them a big hug. It was a very poignant moment for us all.

The ceremony was beautiful, the first of many lovely services of religious dedication that it has been my joy to share. As at any wedding, there were tears shed. Some of the guests, though appreciative of the work of Carmel, still feel it is a waste of a young life to be shut away like that. But my family and close friends shared my joy, as I exchanged the white garments for the serviceable brown serge habit and the white veil of a Novice.

After the ceremony there was the opportunity for me to meet everyone again. They all examined and admired my habit, footwear, brown leather belt and white linen. Everyone asked me to pray for them, and that made me feel dreadfully inadequate. However, I promised that I would. The sisters' prayers will make up for the poverty of mine, I thought – and we hold all things in common.

Then a happy thing happened. Sister Kathleen's brother had recently come to live at Topsham, near Exmouth, with his young wife, and they had come to the ceremony. When they met my sisters and brother, and heard how rarely they were able to see me – this was indeed the first time – they offered to take them to their cottage for the night, so that they could see me again on the morrow. They would then drive them home. Simon wanted to go home with the priest, because he had made other arrangements for the following morning; but Bou and Bridget gladly accepted the offer, and spent that night with Bernard and Lucy. This meant that we could have a good chat the next morning, without all the other friends and well-wishers milling around. Then Lucy drove them all the way back to Ashcott in the afternoon. Today, people think nothing of driving that distance, with fast cars and motorways – I suppose it was about seventy miles; but in 1952 it was still a very long drive. This was the first of many kindnesses that we received from Bernard and Lucy.

For the first few days after taking the Habit the Novice has a more relaxed time, as she gets accustomed to moving around in what is at first a strange garb. You have to learn not to trip over the hem when you go up a step or stairs, for instance, and how to hook it up when you are doing heavy or dirty work. We put on aprons for work – for gardening these were made of sacking – to protect the habits, which we had to take care not to get stained or torn. They were not frequently washed because of the thickness of the material, but were kept well brushed and sometimes hung out to air on the line. They usually looked smart even when they had become very darned and patched after years of wear. Nowadays the cloth is lighter, easily washed and cared for, and not so extensively darned.

I realise as I write this – forty-four years to the day since my Clothing Day – that Sister Kathleen, who made that first habit of mine, is still making the habits for the community! The one I'm wearing today bears the stamp of her careful handiwork. I believe she is making me a new one; she's certainly engaged at the moment in preparing one for the Clothing ceremony which we shall be having soon, as another young postulant takes the next step in her new life. I hope and pray she will be as happy as I have been. This is not to say that there is no suffering – there is no living in love without pain, and often the greater the love the greater the suffering. But there is a very clear distinction between suffering and being miserable. One can suffer deeply – physically, mentally or emotionally – yet underneath the pain there is peace and tranquillity. There is even an amazing happiness – it's hard to put this into words, but those who have experienced it will know what I mean. Because of my nature, and my over-sensitivity, I was to experience suffering, to a greater or lesser degree, a good deal during the course of my life, and no efforts on the part of those around me to prevent or assuage this have been of any avail. Yet all the way along I have known so much joy – in fact, I feel almost ashamed even to mention the suffering when I recall all I have received to fill my heart with happiness and delight.

For the next year life went on more or less in a straightforward manner, and then, a year after my Clothing Day, I made my first Profession. This is really the most important of the steps along the way. It is the true bridal day, the day from which future jubilees are counted. This time the service takes place within the Community, no one from outside being allowed to be present. As in the case of the Clothing, a week's retreat precedes the day. By that time I knew I was in the monastery 'for keeps'. During my first year, even after my Clothing, I sometimes wondered if I was really in the right place; but by the time of my first Profession I knew – at any rate, in so far as it depended on me. No words can describe the joy of that day. It was a day of total giving, as far as my vision could then grasp; and above all, a day of receiving. It was another new beginning, a new life.

It wasn't until the Christmas after my Profession that I saw the family again. The same kind priest must have asked them if they had seen me lately. He was interested in my vocation to the Carmelite way of life, and when he heard that they hadn't seen me since he had taken them to the Clothing he offered to bring them down one day around Epiphany. So we were able to have another lovely day together, and I could see how much they had grown. It was wonderful that this priest should have given them that opportunity of visiting me, because although we didn't know it at the time, the whole community was soon to leave Exmouth and settle in Yorkshire – much too far for any of them to visit.

Over the next year there was talk among the older members of the Community about the increasing volume of traffic day and night along the main road outside the property. Also, the house and garden were getting more and more overlooked as houses were built around us. It was becoming difficult to find the silence that is so important in the kind of life the sisters were trying to lead. In a word, the location was becoming less suitable for a Carmelite monastery. As far as those of us at the younger end of the Community were concerned, life went on as usual. I was learning new skills, and beginning to take on duties that involved me in the daily running and maintenance of the house and garden. I helped with the making of vestments – very pleasant though demanding work. The elderly sister in charge of that department could still produce exquisite needlework, and I found it impossible to match up to, or even approach it; but as the work was to be sold, it had to be perfect. I also worked in the garden, and began to help with the catering, a job I have had on and off for most of my time in Carmel. Another task I much loved was helping the Infirmarian to care for the older or sick sisters.

Life was full and busy, and I was gradually growing into it and plumbing more of its depths. The main work of the house was, of course, prayer, and everything else was subservient to this – everything led to prayer and from it. The monastery bell rang many times every day, and late at night, to call the sisters to the chapel. It was rung for meals, too, and for anything we were all going to do together. Although there were a few clocks around, no one had a watch. They were considered an unnecessary luxury. In my early days as a nun there were still some hour-glasses in use, to measure smaller spaces of time. Today, I think all the sisters have watches; but the bell is still rung.

I could write a book about the sisters who were my companions! Each one was so different, as no doubt you would find in any Carmel. They had all come from such varied backgrounds, had entered at different ages, and done widely diverse jobs before that – usually nothing remotely resembling what they found themselves doing in the monastery. Most, it is true, had entered in their early twenties; but there were some who had come earlier and some later, one in her fifties. Sister Mary had entered at seventeen, straight from school. Today, postulants are not accepted so young, but in those days it was quite common. Some had been teachers, some nurses, one a doctor; one was a librarian, others were business girls. It has been like this all down the centuries. In one way it is a miracle in itself that such differing characters can live together in harmony for their whole lives! But therein, I guess, lies the secret of the Christian message.

Some I didn't really get to know for a long time, either because my work didn't throw me into their company often, or because of their or my natural shyness. I suppose we never do really get to know another person fully. They go on surprising us all their lives! But we were all good friends, and our very differences meant that we learned much from one another, as well as having our rougher edges rubbed off!

130

During my first year after Profession we celebrated, with the whole country, the Queen's coronation. King George VI, her father, had died not long before. Sister Raphael and I decorated the refectory for the occasion. My idea was to put paper streamers and flags around; but Sister Raphael gathered armfuls of pink roses and spread them all over the tables and window ledge. They looked stunning, and their scent filled the house. The provisor found little room left on the tables whereon to bestow her bounty; but apart from that everyone agreed that the room was lovely. It was such a change from its usual functional and austere appearance. Raphael was also a Novice, and although she was much older in years we got on well together.

As time went by the Prioress and her Council began seriously to consider the possibility of moving the Community to a quieter and more remote location. Pictures of houses for sale were obtained and examined carefully. Mother Mary of St John felt very drawn to finding a place in her native Yorkshire. There were already a number of Carmels in the south-west, but only one in the whole of Yorkshire – and that was in the more southern part of the county, near Sheffield. One house was actually decided on, but then for some reason or other it fell through. Perhaps it was too expensive. Several other properties were on the market at the time, so eventually the Prioress and Sister Mary went up to Yorkshire to look at them and assess their suitability.

They were given hospitality by the IBVM nuns in York, who became great friends. From there they were able to visit the various houses. I think the nuns themselves had a car; at any rate someone drove them around. They looked at several which had seemed promising in the brochures, but which proved to be useless for their purpose.

After one fruitless journey, their driver said to them, 'Do come and look at this lovely place; I've just heard that it's up for sale. It's called Thicket Priory, and in years gone by there was a monastery on the site'. Our Prioress and her companion were getting tired by then, and their hopes of finding the right place were fading. They weren't keen to go; but the car was already turning off up the long drive. Soon they caught sight of the building, through the trees. It was a large, beautiful place, built in mellowed brick with stone facings and mullions; old, but not so old as to be decrepit – about one hundred years old, strongly built. It had a couple of towers, one with a clock on it, and it nestled among acres of fields and copses, miles from anywhere. A great atmosphere of peace seemed to enfold it.

Our two got out of the car, went to the door, and made enquiries; but the price of the big sprawling building with so much land was far beyond what they could pay. They were limited to what we could get for our Exmouth house.

So they drove back to the Convent at York, and thought no more about the place that had so captivated them at first sight. However, the following day the Convent phone rang. A voice enquired whether the two nuns from Exmouth were still there. When Sister Mary Joseph went to answer it, she found it was the owners of Thicket Priory. They said they would rather the sisters had their house than anyone else, because they felt that then it would be loved and cared for. They were prepared to negotiate the price according to what we would be able to pay. It was a generosity that will never be forgotten.

Now we could put a name to where we were going and the whole affair seemed, and indeed was, miraculous. Our going there would be a kind of homecoming for the house and land after the hundreds of years that had passed since the nuns in the original monastery on that site had been driven out at the Reformation.

The two travellers returned home, and told us all about their search and miraculous find. We saw photos of our future home, asked innumerable and quite unanswerable questions, and gradually got used to the idea that soon we would be leaving our monastery and venturing forth on what would obviously be a very great undertaking. Moving house, even from a small one to another, is always a big job. Moving a monastery, despite its apparently few possessions, is a daunting task. It would be difficult enough today, but it was very much more so then. One of the things you need to remember when hearing about life at that time is that plastic had not come into general use. Everything was made of natural materials – wood, metal, glass, pottery, etc., and therefore so much

132

of the household equipment in any establishment was much heavier to carry around than it is today. The washing-up tub which we used there (and indeed for many years at Thicket) was made of wood with iron bands round, like part of a barrel but oval in shape.

Mother Mary of St John and her assistant went again to York to see to the business side of the purchase and make the final arrangements. The rest of us made preparations in whatever sphere of work fell to our particular lot. No one knew quite when the move would take place; but at least we knew where we were going. From that moment onwards, things began to move – not rapidly, but steadily. Prospective buyers came to look over the Exmouth house – not that the house would have been of much use, knocked around as it had been to transform it from a 'gentleman's residence' into a monastery for fifteen nuns. But the situation, with the garden bounded by two roads, was right for development. We heard subsequently that the house and chapel had been completely demolished, and new houses built there. In a way it was a relief to learn this. Both house and chapel had been dear to us, holy places sanctified by prayer, laughter and tears. We would have felt sad had they been left to fall into decay. As it was, new families would occupy the garden and house-land; life would carry on and lots of people would enjoy the nearness to the sea. For we were quite near it, though we couldn't actually see it. At night when there were storms at sea we could plainly hear the hollow boom of a bell-buoy warning sailors of dangerous underwater rocks.

During that time I received a letter from home, telling me that my granny had died. This was my mother's mother. She and Grandad used to come and stay with us sometimes for a holiday. She was a warm, loving person, with a great sense of humour, and like her daughter a great reader. She it was who first introduced us to *Three Men in a Boat*. She was, amongst other things, a wonderful cook; during the war she cooked for a big boys' school in the area.

She had grown up at the end of the last century in what may well be the smallest village in Northamptonshire – at least, it was considered so then, called Brockhall. Her father had been stud groom on Earl Spenser's Estate, and even to his old age if he were rubbing or polishing anything, such as his shoes, from sheer force of habit he would make the comforting zizzing noise that he used when grooming his beloved horses. Granny was the youngest of a large family and often used to play with the children who lived at the big house, also called Brockhall. She loved to look back at those days. She shared lessons given by their governess to those children and learned with them to play the organ. Her mother had come from a very musical family who owned a boot-manufacturing business. She also used to take turns with the children in riding what must have been one of the first bicycles after the penny-farthing – a fearsome machine, but they loved it.

When she was old enough, Granny was apprenticed to a prestigious firm of tailors and dressmakers in Northampton. She had to live on the premises, along with the other apprentices, with a supervisor to chaperone them. Her parents had to pay for this training; but it stood her in good stead. She became a superb dressmaker. Soon after the apprenticeship was completed, she married Grandpa, who worked in the boot and shoe trade – Northampton and around there was *the* boot and shoe-making area in those days. There were no trade unions then, or sick pay, and if he were not well, or work was slack, they found it hard to manage. Granny's skill with her needle and sewing-machine saved the situation more than once. My mother could remember her father looking in admiration at an overcoat his wife had just completed, and saying, 'What a garment, Mother!'

They settled in Wellingborough, which is where my mother and her sister were born and brought up, and where Granny lived for the rest of her life. A little coincidence occurred, or rather was discovered, many years later when Julian was married. Mother was talking to his wife, Judy, who came from Kent. Judy told Mother that she also had lived in Northamptonshire as a baby. 'But you probably wouldn't know the place – it was a tiny village called Flore'. 'Why, that was where my mother was christened - in Flore church!' exclaimed Mother. 'And so was I!', said Judy.

I apologise for this digression, but I hope it may be of interest. It is time now to tell you of what in later years we used to refer to as 'The Exodus from Exmouth'.

chapter seventeen

The Exodus from Exmouth

At the time, I was in my last year of Novitiate and the only novice. Mother Mary of St John had been away in York for what seemed to me a very long time. She was both my Prioress and my Novice Mistress, and I missed her greatly. In the course of the negotiations for the new house she had fallen, while at the IBVM Convent, and had fractured her pelvis; so she was gone much longer than planned.

We had been expecting the move for weeks – we had told our families not to write until we were able to give them the new address. Some time in June had been envisaged, but as usually happens with moves there were various delays, and it was nearly the end of July when the time really came.

That was a very hot summer, so hot that even sitting in a 'cool' place to say my Office I could feel the perspiration trickling down my face. The Habits were thicker in those days; there were no thinner ones for summer. But the advantage of the hot weather was that every day was dry and things could be left outside, both before and after we reached Thicket.

Pickford's men came a few days beforehand to see how much furniture there was to move, and assess how many vans they would need. To them, the house looked so bare that they underestimated and afterwards had to increase the number. We all worked hard at the packing, labelling, and sorting – some of the labels were very funny. 'Extern Umbrella' was one. We were taking everything, even light bulbs and built-in cupboards. Sister Teresa carefully dismantled the latter and packed them for reassembly, plastering up any holes made in the walls, and generally trying to leave the house in a reasonable state, even though we knew it might well be demolished before long. We kept a bonfire going, and anything that really looked as if it wouldn't be of use in our new home was consigned to the flames. The only thing we intended to leave behind was a big, heavy, old garden roller which had been on the premises when the Carmel was founded. Its handle was broken, and no one was strong enough to move it. However, Pickford's men must have spotted it, and it was one of the first things we saw when we reached Thicket!

It was a very poignant moment when the Blessed Sacrament was removed from the Tabernacle after Mass on Sunday by the Parish Priest. It brought home to us the reality of the fact that we were truly leaving Exmouth Carmel.

All the things that had to be left to the last minute were packed into Pickford's largest van, the 'Gentle Giant'. The chapel altar went in that, also the mattresses – and the hens! These were in coops and provided with food and water; the lorry men were to give them more supplies en route. There were no motorways in those days and the journey with those huge vehicles could not be completed in one day. The mattresses were the large, heavy, strawpacked Carmelite ones. The sheets, made of serge, were fixed to tapes at the lower end. We each had to put our pillow and any blanket we felt we might need onto the bed, fold the sheets over them, and tie the whole firmly to the mattress. The idea was that when we reached Thicket each person would have her bed complete, ready for the first night.

The removal men thought it all a bit odd. The mattresses were so heavy and awkward that they became weary of carrying them down the stairs and began instead to heave them over the banisters into the hall below. This was good fun for them, but somewhat disastrous to our careful tying up of first-night bedding, as well as damaging some of the mattress stitching, which dated back to 1926 and earlier. One man called out to his mate: 'this one's losing its jacket!' as somebody's bundle of sheets began to come adrift.

Everything began to disappear into the vans, and good friends lent us a few basic necessities that could be used right up to the last minute when everything else had gone. We labelled these carefully, to make sure that they reached their rightful owners at the end of the day. 'Betty's jug', 'Bernard and Lucy's dustpan', etc. helped us over the last day. Sister Teresa had saved a number of jam jars, which we used as cups for our last meal, and could leave behind. We had sandwiches, which didn't need plates. Sister Mary had planned everything with great care and efficiency.

Bernard and Lucy had lent us, amongst other things, a comfortable mattress. This was placed on the floor of the infirmary, and sisters could have a little rest on it if they were in need, on that last long day; for there were no beds left in the house by then, or even a blanket, and we were not leaving until nearly midnight.

Towards the end of the day, a couple of us went all around checking up to make sure nothing was left that should come with us, or be thrown away. In the garden shed we found a bottle with a little fluid in it. There was no label, so we tipped the fluid into the bonfire. Alas, it was Sister Teresa's little bottle of turpentine, which she was keeping to the very end so as to be able to clean the paint off her hands before we set out. I remember feeling miserable about it; but knowing her I expect she devised some other method for getting the paint off before the time of departure came.

It was after 11 p.m. by the time the cars arrived to take us to Exeter station. We each carried a bag containing our breviaries and some sandwiches; and our folded cloaks on our arms. A few chosen souls, noted for great trustworthiness, carried the sacred vessels from the sacristy, wrapped in parcels and tied to their belts with string so that there was no possibility of losing them on the way. It so happened that earlier in the evening Sister Catherine had found a good pair of clogs that had been left behind – too good for the bonfire, and with plenty of wear left in them. So she wrapped them up into a manageable package and decided to carry that as well as her bag.

Bernard, Sister Kathleen's brother, drove one car, and our friend, Betty, the other. Betty had taken her aged mother, well into her eighties, to the station beforehand so that she could see this sight of the nuns' departure, and wish them well.

The car journey through the silent villages was an unforgettable experience for us. Was it moonlight, or just the kind of summer night that is never really dark? There was a strange, dreamlike quality about gliding through those Devonshire villages, many with thatched cottages and little twinkling lights. Even the names, new to us, added glamour – Countess Wear was one I remember. Sister Kathleen found it hard to speak naturally to her brother who was driving, because of this strangeness and beauty, and the fact that we were all out of the enclosure the first time, for some sisters, for many years.

The idea of travelling overnight was that we should be able to get some rest during the journey and then have plenty of daylight hours left when we reached York. Trains were still at that time (1955) powered by steam. The carriages had separate compartments, each seating about six or eight people, with a corridor running alongside. We had booked two compartments.

The train left about midnight. We said our last goodbyes to our kind friends on Exeter station, and walked along the platform in solemn procession, Sister Teresa leading, carrying the Cross. Thus we boarded the train and settled ourselves into the compartments. I was in the one in which Sister Mary was in charge – I expect they thought I needed careful watching!

Then off we sped, through the darkened countryside, Taunton next stop, so near my home! Then Bridgwater, nearer still, flashed past. Sister Mary's head raised a bit. 'Bridgwater, Sister Elizabeth', she said kindly. She little knew what was going on inside me; but I beamed as cheerfully as I could. Then on and on and on – trains didn't go as fast in those days – until we reached London around 8 a.m.

A delightful extern sister from Notting Hill Carmel met us at the station, and helped us over the next stage of the journey, which was to cross part of London to get to Kings Cross for the train north. She had arranged taxis but there was very little time so we had to go at break-neck speed.

Sister Teresa always carried the processional Cross at Community ceremonies, so she deemed it her great privilege to carry this Cross personally from the doorstep of Exmouth Carmel to its place at Thicket Carmel. She never let go of it during the whole journey, proudly holding it aloft on the railway stations despite the astonished stares of the passers-by!

The Kings Cross to York train was the last lap of our journey. We ate our sandwiches as we sped out of London into what was,

138

to me, the unknown north. For some of the others, it had a sense of home-coming. After the night travel of the first train, it was good to be going along in sunshine, so that we could look out of the windows. I've always recalled with delight that as the train drew into York station there was a garden beside the line with the word YORK formed in flowers.

There on the station were some of the IBVM nuns, waiting to welcome us with so much love and care. They had even hired taxis to take us the tiny distance from the station to their Convent.

At the time they still had a flourishing school; but this was the beginning of the summer holidays, so all the girls had gone home. We were taken first into what seemed to us a luxuriously-furnished parlour, where we sat on the floor – naturally! – on the thick pile carpet. Those of us who were carrying the sacred vessels explained what they were, and why they could not be put down unless in an absolutely safe place. The Sisters took them with great care to a place of safety. They came to Sister Catherine, who was still holding her parcel of clogs. 'Let me relieve you of your precious burden', said a kindly sister, reverently reaching out for the package. Sister Catherine did not have the heart to enlighten her at that moment, so the clogs were put carefully with the chalices and pyxes.

Then the sisters showed us to a wash room, with a row of little sinks – they knew how much we were longing for a wash and freshen-up. We felt so hot and sticky. There had been no hot water all the previous day for washing, so we'd had to do our best with cold before the journey.

As soon as we were all refreshed and more comfortable – the weather was exceedingly hot – we were taken to a dining-room where a lovely lunch was prepared. I can't remember all that was provided, but I know they gave us very delicate and beautifully-cooked fish, knowing that we didn't eat meat, and Reverend Mother had especially chosen raspberries for our dessert, because she felt they would be cooling. We were waited on like queens.

After the meal, the sisters showed us around the house and school. We admired the portraits of Mary Ward and many of the early sisters from old English families. Then there were the relics, such as St Margaret Clitherow's hand. We saw also many sacristy treasures – heavily embroidered 'fiddle-back' vestments, a huge gem-encrusted monstrance, never used because of its great weight; and lots of other interesting things. In the chapel there was a place where the floor-boards could be lifted to expose the entrance to a priests' hiding-hole. But we were anxious, by then, to be on our way. The IBVM nuns' kindness to us was to extend over many years.

We looked out eagerly as we drove through the quiet, sunlit villages, and up the long drive – and there it lay: Thicket, our new home, looking very solid with its warm red brick and mullioned windows. It was the feast of St Anne, 26th July 1955, about four o'clock in the afternoon.

We got out of the cars and formed into procession again, first putting on our cloaks. The three sisters who were already there came out to join us. There was a white side gate, in those days, under a huge cedar of Lebanon. Through this we processed, the Cross still leading the way, along the south terrace and in at the door on the east side of the house. As we went we chanted the traditional *Laudate Dominum, omnes gentes* on monotone.

The Sisters who had gone ahead of us had done a mammoth job, making sure that each sister had a cell with her bed in it for when darkness fell. There was no electricity; this didn't come for a long time. But there was mains water, and we had a primus stove, which Sister Mary Bernard soon got going in the kitchen. A room had been planned for the chapel and sacristy, and for the community room. So it was already Carmel; and though that was the end of our journey, it was the beginning of a whole new life.

chapter eighteen

Thicket Priory

Hundreds of years before we arrived at Thicket Priory there had been nuns living a very similiar life to ours on that very spot. Although their monastery was destroyed and the sisters disbanded, the area continued to bear the name Thicket Priory all down the years. A large dwelling house was built on the site as time went by, but this was destroyed by fire. I think it was in the 1840s that a new house was erected, built as a stately Victorian home, in the days of plenty of servants and a whole team of gardeners. The main rooms were spacious and imposing, with high ceilings – one of them beautifully embossed. This room became our choir, which is what our part of the chapel is always referred to in Carmel. It is where we sing God's praise often through the day. Workmen were already engaged on necessary alterations to provide access to this room.

The first floor also had some large and beautiful rooms, which had been the principal bedrooms. These we arranged to use as the various offices of the house, such as the linen room and the robe room (where the habits are made), the vestment room, and the library. Upstairs again were smaller rooms, some of which had been built as servants' quarters.

Then there were outbuildings which had been coach-houses and stables for the horses, all solidly built and pleasing to the eye. There was a clock tower, with a big clock that struck the hours, once we had discovered how to wind it up – and who was nimble enough to climb up inside the narrow tower to do so. There were other towers, too, one with little rooms in it which made compact and rather lovely cells, in time. One small tower, that looked romantic from the outside, was in fact simply the kitchen chimney.

The house stood on a raised terrace, from which steps led down to a wide grassy area which must originally have been a velvet green lawn. It was rough grass when we arrived, but with its own wild beauty. On one side it sloped down to a lake with tree-lined edges, wild water-lilies on its quiet surface, and moorhens, coots and other water-birds in residence. The whole garden had obviously been carefully landscaped. There were many magnificent trees of various kinds, planted so as to provide vistas of great beauty and serenity from whichever direction one looked.

There were two bridges that crossed the lake in different places – it was a long lake of varying widths, and the bridges spanned the narrower parts. One had to cross the main, stone-built bridge in order to reach the vegetable garden unless one was prepared (and had the time) to walk all around the side of the lake. That was indeed a wonderful walk, but impracticable for everyday gardening work, when one had to get to the vegetable garden and back in as short a time as possible. Even over the bridge it took five minutes each way, longer if one were pushing a wheelbarrow of vegetables.

But that vegetable garden! It must have been a gardener's paradise when it was well cared for, and even as it was in our time it was a joy to work in. Victorian gardeners knew how to design and build a garden in such a way that all the natural amenities were used to the full. Very high brick walls surrounded it, with greenhouses built against those facing south, where they would get maximum sunlight. On the west-facing side were a hundred or so cordon pears of many varieties, from very early to the latest keepers. On another wall were espalier plum trees, and a damson. There had been a tall vinery once, but this had been dismantled before we got there. There were tool-sheds, and storage houses, cold-frames (these had been damaged while the house had stood empty but we were able to use parts of them), also a partially sunken greenhouse with heating pipes, which must have been used for raising hot-house plants.

The soil in that garden had been worked, manured, and kept in top fettle for a century or more, so it was deep and good, even though it soon became very weedy in parts. There was a cottage beside the vegetable garden; probably the head gardener had lived here. His team of under-gardeners, down to the gardener's boy starting off as little more than a child, would have come in by day from the nearby villages.

However, during those first few days, and even weeks after our arrival, we had little time to stop and gaze at our beautiful surroundings. They unfolded gradually before our eyes as we began to venture around, and had arranged things in the house into some kind of workable order. We needed to get the altar-bread making under way as soon as possible, because this was our livelihood. We used two Primus stoves to cook them on, until the electricity came. Rooms had to be allocated for various purposes – and there was so much cleaning to do! The house had been empty for six months before we came, and birds had found their way in. Jackdaws had made nests – the chimneys had been stuffed with their sticks which had fallen down into the rooms and all over the floors, carrying soot with them. There were dead flies by the pailful. Also, all the floors had previously been carpeted, and as we intended that they should simply be wood – and they were good wood – they needed to be scrubbed clean before they could be stained and waxed.

Everyone pitched in with a will and we gradually got things into place. Of course it took years to get it as it is now – in fact, as in any home, there are jobs that still need doing.

We did not yet have electricity. The previous owners had had a generator, but this had fallen into desuetude, and even if we had been able to get it repaired the wiring would all have needed replacing. Sister Catherine's family, who lived in Lancashire, asked her what they could bring us that would help us in our new home. She suggested an oil-lamp. When they came to visit us, they had been round all their friends and collected lamps of every shape and size, which they proudly presented, complete with instructions as to how they all worked! They proved to be a godsend, because as autumn came on and the days grew shorter we needed a lot of lights around the house. We had two beautiful Aladdin lamps for the choir. These gave a soft, clear light, so different from electric bulbs, which can be very glaring. These kind people had even brought some of the tiny lamps such as we had had in our bedrooms as children. They were particularly useful standing in corners of dark passages, and at the top of the stairs.

Although there was so much to be done, and not many of us to do it, we were very careful not to let all the work stand in the way of our times of prayer. Sometimes it was tempting to finish off a job before laying down our tools; but here our training over the years came to our rescue. When the bell rang for prayer, we stopped. And indeed it was a relief to be able to forget all about the work for that precious hour, or however long it was, and settle quietly for our time of prayer. While the glorious summer weather lasted, some of us would slip off into the garden and find a quiet nook there. One of the things we all noticed about the Priory, and especially about the garden, was the atmosphere of tranquillity and prayer. It was quite remarkable. We felt that the nuns who had lived and died there, and were buried somewhere in the grounds, were welcoming us to the place that they, too, had hallowed with their prayer and faithful living out of their consecration. There was a great peace.

Quite early on we realised that the altar-bread work would not bring in sufficient money both to keep us and to pay for the alterations that needed doing to the house. So we went in for hens in a big way. There was plenty of land, and good outbuildings. We had a sister who was an expert carpenter, so she designed and made perches, nest-boxes, and feeding-troughs with wood and hardboard. We bought day-old chicks, darling little fluffy balls, and reared them ourselves.

While they were tiny, the chicks were kept in the house in one of the upstairs rooms, in a special brooder with a paraffin heater underneath. Each day the brooder had to be cleaned out, and a fresh piece of sacking put in for the little chicks to nestle on. One day, Sister Mary and Sister Catherine went up as usual to do this job – it needed two people, because the chicks were like little mice, running around all over the place, and one had to be very adroit or else they'd all get out into the room, and be impossible to catch. On this day, Sister Catherine suddenly sprang up. 'Oh–ooh!' she squealed, clutching at her clothing and wriggling about frantically. 'One's gone up my sleeve!' A chick had run up the inside of her sleeve and into the top of her habit, tickling all the way up. After a bit she extricated it while Mary got on with the work, slightly disapproving of her having made an apparently childish fuss about such a small thing. Catherine returned to the job, but a few minutes later the boot was on the other foot – up leaped Mary, clutching at her sleeve, then her neck – one of the chicks had done the same for her, and as she was even more ticklish than Catherine, she made more of a fuss! So they both had a great laugh together, and recounted the story to us at recreation that evening. That's one thing that you really do need in our kind of life, and I think we have all got it – a sense of humour! You have to be able to see the funny side of life, and not take yourself too seriously either.

We had many adventures with the hens – enough to fill several books! We kept some of them outdoors, where they scratched around under the trees and cleared the ground admirably. The rest were in houses, on what was known as deep litter. When we first started that system and the Prioress was discussing it with us, old Sister Anne said, 'that *will* be good for them'. 'However did you know about deep litter?' asked the Prioress, knowing that Anne had been in Carmel for many years, and had never moved in poultry circles even before that. 'Oh, I thought you said beef liquor', chuckled Sister Anne, who was getting slightly hard of hearing.

Poor Anne had fallen in the garden just before we left Exmouth, and broken her hip; she was eighty-five at the time. Hip replacements had not yet been developed so although she was in hospital for a long time she was never able to walk again. She lived to be ninety, and entered fully into all we did at Thicket from her wheel-chair or bed. Her mind was perfectly clear, her wit quick, and her dear old fingers still able to do her needlework right up to the end. She knew about so many things – she was an expert on wild flowers and delighted in each new specimen I brought in from the garden for her to identify. She was always so interested in everything. One day, when she was nearly ninety, she asked me to explain some detail about the layout of the house. When I had finished she thanked me graciously – Sister Anne was always gracious and grateful for the least thing – and said: 'I'm so glad you've told me that. I do like to learn something new every day'. From someone of her age, I felt that this was a real lesson for me and I have treasured the memory ever since. That was how she kept so young at heart, despite her physical disability. Another thing she once said to me – to add to my store of treasures – was: 'it's the *little* things that matter. The *big* things will take care of themselves'.

Sisters Kathleen, Catherine and I were the three youngest and strongest in the house, so the main work and management of the hen business was placed in our hands. We became experts on all aspects of poultry-keeping. It was hard work, but for me at any rate it was quite congenial, despite the mess one sometimes got in, and the pungent smell of hen-manure that clung to one's garments! I think some of the others found it more of a chore; but we knew why we were doing it, and as with all the other work we put our hearts into it. St Teresa once said, 'what does it matter in which way we serve?' This was a service to the Community and therefore to God, and we were happy to render it.

People around us soon came to know of our arrival and were most helpful. Not many actually lived nearby, but because of our church connections with York and Selby, we soon had a number of kind friends. Some came to help us manually, joining in the painting and scrubbing. Others arranged fund-raising events, and brought us the proceeds. A little group of ladies from York came every Saturday afternoon for years, helping us with the hens, or whatever needed to be done that day. They not only gave their time and energies but something even more precious, which they themselves were not aware of at the time – encouragement. Everyone needs a little of this, at least now and again, and Carmelites are no exception. Our helpers were so convinced of the value of what we were doing, both as to the setting up of the monastery and of course the life and aim of the sisters, that their enthusiasm and keenness provided the affirmation we needed. Before too long we really began to feel we were an accepted part of the local scene.

One of our fund-raising friends, Paddy, came one day in great excitement, and asked to see the Prioress at once, if at all possible. Mother Mary John went to the door and there stood Paddy, his eyes shining with pleasure at the news he was bringing. One of the most famous footballers of the day was coming to York – 'and he's a Catholic!' Mother looked at him, partly picking up his enthusiasm, but also partly very puzzled. He broke into her silence.

'But he might give you a FOOTBALL!' he burst out. Poor Mother Mary John looked more bemused than ever. What could *we* do with a football?

So he then had to explain to his uncomprehending friend that if this top player were to sign a football, it could be raffled and bring in money for Carmel.

That episode was only one of many. I think it was Paddy who organised, during our first springtime there, the picking of baths and pails full of daffodils to sell on the market for Mothers' Day. The Thicket daffodils have to be seen to be believed. The banks of the lake, the copses, the wide spaces under the huge, ancient trees – in spring they all become golden and glorious with daffodils. There are lots of different varieties, so that the season extends through from the early ones to the latest – usually the pheasant-eye narcissi. Like Wordworth's beside the lake, they have filled the inward eye of so many who have been at Thicket in the spring.

They are by no means the only spring flowers, though. I met again there all the treasures of my childhood wood-lands, free to spread and bloom as they chose in that semi-wild garden. One I hadn't known before, the dainty wood-sorrel, became a special joy for me. They did so well in that soil, which also supported azaleas and stupendous rhododendrons.

We too began to put down roots again after our transplanting from Exmouth, and to grow and flourish in our Yorkshire home and garden.

The Community at prayer in the Choir at Thicket Priory

Cutting altar bread into individual hosts

chapter nineteen

New recruits

The first Community ceremony that took place at Thicket was my final Profession. It was on the first of May, 1956, and was a wonderful occasion for me, and indeed for us all. We always find that when a new Sister makes her first or final Profession it is a moment of renewal for all of us. With the newly-professed, each one in the silence of her heart makes again that total gift of self that she had made with so much love on her own bridal day. Carmel is a land of loving.

There was not a large crowd to attend the ceremony. For one thing, the temporary chapel was very small; and for another we did not as yet know many people in the area. None of my family were able to come. Yorkshire is a very long way from Somerset. In fact, I wondered then if I ever should see them again! But, of course, in due time, I did, though it was not for some years. The first one to be able to visit me was Bou, and what a joy that was!

Bou was by then doing the job I had done – teaching at the Glastonbury convent school, and loving every minute. She had always been – and still is – wonderful with children. She came and stayed a few days at Thicket, joining in with the painting and various other jobs, and chatting with me in between. I was able to hear all the family details that didn't find their way into letters; and she was so happy to be able to see my new surroundings, so that she could picture me wherever she was, and could describe it all to my parents and the rest of the family.

A year or two later, Bridget came. She was still studying at the Minehead convent school, but partly teaching there as well – she was what was then known as a pupil-teacher. She had grown from a thirteen-year-old to a young lady and her long plaits had gone. In place of them she wore her hair in what looked to me a most unkempt style – as if someone with raggedly cut short hair had just got out of bed. I learned later that this was the latest fashion in young hair-styles! Coming to Yorkshire was the longest journey she had made on her own, and she was quite proud of it. She, too, came along to help a bit – she came out to the hen-yard, and borrowed a big sacking apron from one of the sisters. I thought that being a country girl like me, she wouldn't mind helping with the mucking-out. It was only much later that I found out that she was really quite fastidious, and unlike her sister preferred to keep her hands clean! At the time, she valiantly undertook the task, and did it very well.

After that, I didn't get any more visits from home until Simon drove up in his pride and joy: a second-hand green van (cheaper than a car). With him was his even greater treasure – his young wife. You can imagine how much I loved seeing them both – I had heard all about the wedding, and seen some photos, but actually meeting Margaret in person was incalculably better. I was able to show them around a bit, and they were keen to see and hear all they could. Simon was twenty-three and Margaret nineteen; but they both looked so very young, like teenagers.

About that time we received our first Yorkshire postulant, Teresita. She had been visiting us as a helper, with a group of friends. She didn't tell us that in her heart she had felt the calling to become a nun for some time. We thought she was just a particularly devoted helper. Then one day she confided to the Prioress that she wanted to become a Carmelite. This was a joy for us all because no one had joined us since I had come. Teresita had a lovely singing voice, as well as many other gifts. Before long she gave up her job, parted with all her possessions, and entered Carmel.

Meanwhile we had seen several spring-times and all the other seasons as they passed by, and in each discovered new delights we hadn't found before. There were so many flowering shrubs, unusual trees, and of course wild flowers in profusion. One of the first big garden jobs we did was to plant an apple-orchard. We had had some trees given us, and we added to these, choosing varieties that would in time keep us in apples for most of the year. When these little trees began to blossom they were a lovely sight; and as the orchard was near the house the Sisters working or sitting in the

150

rooms on that side of the house had the full benefit of their beauty.

In 1960, Sister Anne died, the first to be laid to rest in our own cemetery in the grounds. We missed her sadly, yet we had known that we couldn't have had her much longer as she was ninety, and very frail. Soon after her passing I received a letter from Bridget, telling me that on the advice of the sisters at the Minehead school she was going to a teacher training college in Salford. She was a born teacher, they said, and should acquire the qualifications then deemed necessary for the work. She promised to come over to Thicket to see me, in the spring.

It was a long, cold winter, or so it seemed to me. Yorkshire winters were very different from those we had experienced at Ashcott, with its sheltered, more southerly climate. However, at last a softer wind began to blow, and the daffodils raised their golden trumpets to proclaim the spring. The little 'lent lilies' always appeared first, as if to test the air before the others put forth their blooms. Bridget wrote to say that she was bringing her friend, a fellow-student at the college. This girl was thinking about becoming a nun, possibly a Carmelite, and would like to have a chat with our Prioress.

We provided a good meal for them when they arrived, knowing that students are always hungry – I was provisor at the time, and had to arrange the meals, both for ourselves and for visitors. Then later in the day, as I was the youngest sister and not too busy in the afternoons, I was deputed to take Bridget and Sylvia round the grounds, so that they could get an idea of what it was all like. Naturally I was thrilled to do this. To be able to walk with Bridget again was a joy I had certainly never expected to have!

The two girls were eager to see everything. I took them across the bridge and along the far side of the lake where the daffodils were just beginning to open. A large tree had recently fallen there, and we had had to get a man in to saw the stump off cleanly, and get the branches out of the water.

'You can tell the age of the tree by counting the rings', said one of them brightly. Then the two ran down the slope to the water's edge, where the sawn stump remained. They were such pretty girls, and I watched them, with their college scarves flying out, and their hair tossed by the wind. The picture of that moment impressed itself deeply on my memory. I thought that if either or both of them ever did become Carmelites, I should always remember that scene.

To my amazement and delight, not only did Sylvia decide she would enter at Thicket, but Bridget too had felt the call to give up her teaching and become a nun. So, within a few years, we had two more recruits. Sylvia was only eighteen, and her parents very sensibly asked her to complete her teacher training course first, so that if it turned out that her vocation was not for Carmel she could get a job as a teacher without delay. Bridget was already twenty-one, and so was free to do as she wished – this was before coming-of-age was lowered to eighteen.

She wrote home, explaining very simply that she had decided not to continue at the College, but to join me in Carmel. She was much more sensible than I had been! So when she went home for the Easter holidays, everyone there knew what her plans were and they made no fuss; they accepted it wonderfully, even though it must have been very hard for them all.

Bridget's coming began a new chapter for me. She was twenty-one and I nearly thirty-one. Although we were sisters we had to keep all the rules regarding silence, so I often didn't get a chance to talk with her for weeks at a stretch. There is, however, a way in which one can communicate without a word spoken. A glance, a gesture, simply a presence, can convey more sometimes than books full of words. We were living and working in the same house, sitting at meals in the refectory, singing in the chapel together. All this makes for a depth of communication often not possible with words. I must admit that her training in the Novitiate cost me more than my own had. I felt it dreadfully if I thought she was having a difficult time. It was foolish of me, really, because in all probability the things I thought she would find most difficult or painful, and therefore suffered over myself, were not those which cost her most dear. But I felt for her so much, and feared that she might be tempted to give up before she had discovered the true meaning and joy of the life. I had been like a second mother to her at home, and part of me had not as yet relinquished that motherly hold. I went through a lot of unnecessary suffering in consequence. It had the advantage of making me pray a great deal for my little sister.

When the time came for her Clothing ceremony we were able to invite Father's brother and his wife. They had always been good to us – in fact, it was they who gave me, at my request, my first Bible. Simon's young wife had given us her beautiful wedding-gown, so Bridget wore that, and subsequently Sylvia did too. Not long after that, the ceremony was changed and the white bridal clothes used no more.

I was deeply thrilled that Bridget should have become a Carmelite, because I knew she would experience great happiness and what is known today as 'fulfilment', and in those days 'self-abandonment', which I suppose are in spite of the apparent contradiction two sides of the same coin. True happiness lies in giving, and the greater joy in the more complete giving. St Augustine says somewhere that we have to be wholly emptied of ourselves in order to be filled with love. I think I know what he means.

Now that two of us were in Carmel, our parents began writing – not long letters, but so very precious to us both. Gradually we had all flown from the home nest, except Julian. Bou had married a childhood friend of Simon's, and gone out to Africa, where David's work for the World Health Organisation necessitated his moving around quite often. This meant that they were never long at one address. Their first three children were born in Africa; but the climate was not very suitable for little English children. After a few years they returned to Somerset, to the great delight of our parents, and have lived there ever since.

Not long after Bridget and Sylvia joined us we went through a very sad period. At the time of Sister Anne's death, Sister Teresa had made a huge concrete cross for the cemetery, designing and casting it herself. She was always very clever with her hands, and full of good ideas – quite a remarkable person in fact, good at so many things. She looked after the garden in those early years at Thicket, as well as doing lots of other jobs at the same time. She was not only an accomplished carpenter and joiner but also a gifted needlewoman. Her big, capable hands could both wield hammer and hoe and also create tiny, beautiful objects: miniature Carmelite cells for gifts, soft toys – so many imaginative things. She took a big part in transforming the house into a very suitable and lovely monastery. She was always cheerful and happy; a delightful person to have around. One day, when she was helping me to serve cabbage onto the dinner-plates in the silence of the monastic kitchen, I picked out with a scowl of annoyance a large, cooked caterpillar from the pan. Instantly her twinkling blue eyes met mine. 'No extra charge for those!' she whispered, and my scowl vanished, taking with it all my criticism, and we chuckled together.

When she made that big cross, and helped erect it in the cemetery, no one ever could have guessed that hers would be the next grave to Sister Anne's. She was still in her fifties, rosy-cheeked and energetic. But during the next couple of years she had to go into hospital for what was only a small operation. However, while she was there, tests showed that she was very ill with cancer and could not live more than a few months.

It was a terrible blow for us all, and I remember that Christmas as a very sad one as we saw her failing, yet still trying to keep up her spirit – and ours. Everyone tried to help the others, and the Sisters who worked in the infirmary did their best to find ways of getting her stronger. Medicine had not progressed so far as it has today, so she was not taken into hospital again. She stayed at home, and we did what we could; and when she died we laid her beside Sister Anne, under the shadow of the big cross. It took us all a long time to recover from the sorrow of losing Teresa.

Some time afterwards – it may have been the following summer – Mother made her one and only visit to Carmel. Simon had by then progressed from his little green van to a proper car, which he'd bought from their doctor at home. He and his wife now had a baby son, and they had the wonderful idea of bringing both Mother and the baby to Yorkshire to visit Bridget and me. They wanted to bring Father also, but by then he had become very crippled with arthritis, and though he would dearly have loved to come, he realised that he could never have survived the long journey by car.

154

We cleaned up the little cottage near the vegetable garden, and took down bedding and cookery utensils. People had occasionally stayed there before, but in between we had used it for various purposes, including the rearing of young chicks! However, we got it all clean and bright, though extremely simply furnished. On the day of their arrival we stocked the kitchen with fresh food, and made sure the beds were aired.

People coming up from Somerset today by road would find it hard to believe what a long and tedious journey it was at that time. There were no motorways, and Simon's car was not the fastest, although he was a very careful driver and had planned the route beforehand. They had to travel all day, and it was quite late in the evening when at last they arrived. The Community had already sung Compline, the night prayer of the Church, when Bridget and I walked softly out of the house and through the grounds to the big gate. It was later than we had expected, and we were getting anxious about them. It was a beautiful July evening, the air perfumed with mown grass and many a scented flower. The lime trees were in bloom.

At last we heard a car approaching up the long drive. We opened up the big wooden gates, which were normally kept locked, and there they were – Simon, Margaret, their baby son, and – Mother! I had not seen her for twelve years. Her hair had begun to go grey. It had been so brown and bright when I'd left home; but of course she had only been forty-three then.

At first I felt there was a little tension. It was as if she were still hoping that we might both change our minds, and decide to come home again. But that melted away before long. We only stayed with them briefly that evening, just long enough to settle them into the cottage and show them where things were. Then we scampered back to the monastery and crept indoors to bed.

The sisters had kindly arranged to help out with our work, so that we might have plenty of time to be with our visitors. They all knew that this was a very special visit. Most of them had visits from their families occasionally, but as ours lived so far away it was for us a rare occurrence. Indeed, Mother never made the long journey again.

She was eager to see all she could – she couldn't get over all the hens, and the baskets of brown eggs. At home all the small farms, and other people as well, had chickens, pecking around the garden and outside the farmhouse door; but there would usually be no more than a dozen, or at most twenty. The sight of hundreds, all scratching about in the litter and under the trees, was something she had never seen before.

Simon and Margaret were also taking it all in, and the baby, Stephen, although only seven months old, examined everything with apparently intense interest. During the times when Bridget and I were occupied in the monastery, they made themselves at home in the cottage, and sometimes came up to the chapel.

They stayed two or three days, and then had to return home, because Simon was working at the bank, and Mother had her music pupils. The great thing about that visit was that it helped Mother to see that we were both happy in our life in Carmel, and were in good health, and contented. Mothers always do worry about their offspring, and she was no exception. I think that being able to see her daughters again, and their surroundings, dispelled a few erroneous ideas, and paved the way for a greater acceptance of our vocation. I don't know that she ever did accept it fully, as Father did, but at least she felt happier about us both. She was an unselfish person – she wouldn't have wished us to leave Carmel for her own sake; but she feared we would not really be happy.

During the next few years, more postulants joined us. They didn't all stay, but we always feel that each one who comes leaves us the richer for her having been with us; and they themselves derive benefit from their time – even if only very short – in Carmel. The Vatican Council was beginning to come into our lives and thinking. The world around us was changing rapidly, and in a gentler but no less far-reaching way our lives were also being reviewed and renewed. This set the stage for the next crucial event for us all at Thicket.

chapter twenty

Another challenge

At some time during the mid-sixties, Bishop Gordon Wheeler of Leeds, who occasionally visited Thicket, expressed a wish to have a Carmelite monastery in, or near, Leeds. He talked it over with our Prioress; but she knew we could not possibly spare enough sisters to make a new foundation. We only had sufficient to keep our own monastery going and earn the money to pay for the building work that was still not completed. So the matter was left, and no one thought more about it for several years. However, a surprising number of new recruits began to arrive, and the Community grew to twenty-one. We knew at the time a very saintly priest who used to come and give us talks. He had lived and worked in Yorkshire a good deal of his life, and felt it would indeed be a great good if a monastery were to be founded in the Leeds area. So the idea surfaced again.

Meanwhile, Bridget and I had had disturbing news from home. Mother had developed diabetes, and Father had broken his hip. None of their children were at home; Julian was at Cambridge, Bou and Simon both had young children and were unable to help. Carmelites had never been allowed to go home before, for any reason whatsoever. But this was the late 1960s, and rethinking was going on among religious orders. Mother Prioress got in touch with our Bishop, and after much consideration it was decided that as two of us were in Carmel, one should be allowed to go home for just long enough to help our parents over the crisis.

So Bridget made the long journey by bus and train, and was able to minister to their needs. Father had come back from hospital, where his broken hip had been fixed, but he was still very incapacitated and unable to do much for himself. Mother had expected to be able to care for him, but she had had to be taken into hospital herself after a bad diabetic coma.

Bridget was a born nurse and a great organiser, though not very experienced as a cook. But the very fact of her having been allowed to come home and help them was better medicine for them both than anything else in the world, and before long they picked up – in fact, Mother discharged herself from the hospital on the grounds that her daughter had come home to look after her. It was an immense joy for them both to see their 'Queen' again; and indeed for her as well, because neither of us had thought we would ever see our beloved father any more. We knew he could never travel to Yorkshire.

After a couple of weeks Bridget came home to Carmel again, having set them both well on the road to recovery – though of course the diabetes would never be cured. Mother had learned to do her own insulin injections, and to cope with her diet, so the anxiety was allayed to a certain extent. Diabetes is never predictable – there were to be some frightening days over the next years; but Mother had courage, and a great capacity for making the best of even apparently unpromising situations. She was able to help Father – who was also very independent and would only accept help if he realised even he couldn't manage without! So they cared for one another, and learned how to live with the disabilities that the years had brought. Simon and Bou would visit them whenever they could, and take their children. How they loved those visits! The little grandchildren were a source of much joy to them both.

Back at Thicket, discussions were going on about the possibility, and the feasibility, of making a foundation in the Leeds diocese. There were so many things to be taken into consideration, not least finding a suitable property. How would the sisters support themselves? How would we ever be able to afford the initial stages of buying and setting up the house? Which sisters would go?... and many more almost insuperable problems. A lot of prayer, heart-searching, thinking, and listening to advice went on. Apart from anything else, we were a very united and happy Community and none of us could bear the thought that we would have to be separated. Thicket was a beautiful place, and we had all worked hard to make it into a good Carmel. Even though, as nuns, we were ready to go wherever we might be sent, and knew that if the eventuality should arise we would go freely and willingly, it would still be a big wrench humanly speaking. In fact, when the time came we realised just how free we were at heart to go or stay. The new place would still be Carmel, and therefore our home.

But it was no easy task to find the right place for a new monastery. Several houses were looked at, but were found to be quite unsuitable. We needed somewhere with sufficient land for us to be as self-supporting as possible; but we were not keen to saddle ourselves with a big old house that needed a lot of upkeep. It was important for our kind of life that it should be in a quiet place. So the search took some time. A good friend placed her car at our disposal, and took the Prioress and other sisters to inspect the various properties that had been suggested to us.

At that same time, the Bishop had opened an Ecumenical Centre at a large house he had acquired called Wood Hall, not far from Wetherby. This, the first of its kind in England, I believe, was especially committed to implementing the teachings of the Second Vatican Council. It was a combination of Conference Centre and Retreat House, and already excellent speakers from all over the country were giving talks and retreats there. Some sisters from two of the Apostolic Orders worked hard, together with the director, Mgr Michael Buckley, who was a quite remarkable and far-sighted priest, to make this pioneering venture a success. Today, retreat houses are found all over the place, but then it was something not new but rare, particularly with its strong ecumenical basis. Though the director and the sisters were Catholics, the house was used and greatly appreciated by Anglicans, Methodists and others. When we first came to know of it, a chapel was just being built on the hill a little above the main house. It was to be called the Chapel of the Good Shepherd, and was to be for the use of all denominations – hence the name.

It was the Bishop's suggestion that we should visit Wood Hall, and the Prioress and one of our sisters went there. The staff made them most welcome; and before long it was decided that the new Carmel should be built on land adjacent to the partially-built chapel, which it would share. The terrain was steep but could quite easily be levelled, and we envisaged a very modest, one-storey building

– at any rate, to begin with.

Wood Hall itself was an old house. Parts of it were very old indeed, and in the past it had belonged to Mother Mary of St John's family, the Vavasours of Hazlewood. Over the centuries it had been added to, so that it had become a very attractive stately home, though no longer used as such. In recent times, it had been put to various uses. It was a boys' school for some years. In the war it became a maternity home, as did Hazlewood Castle, when the hospitals had enough to cope with caring for wounded servicemen and civilian victims of air raids.

There were builders already on the site, constructing the chapel. So plans were drawn up, and negotiations set in motion. Everything had to be done with the utmost economy, because we couldn't afford to do it in any other way. And that was good – St Teresa herself was very keen that the sisters should never build pretentious monasteries. In fact, she once said that she hoped the day they did such a thing 'the building would fall down around them'! So often, in this country, when a monastery was being founded, the cheapest way had been to buy a large, unwanted house, and adapt it. To build a new monastery could be very costly, considering the size it would need to be. But in this case, because we were only going to be a few sisters to begin with, and as the chapel would be already built, a small bungalow-type house on land belonging to the Church was the most practical option.

So that was the beginning of Wood Hall Carmel. A friend of ours went over to see the foundations being laid, and took with him a little tin full of earth from Thicket's garden. He put this into the base of what was to be our choir. During the months while the building was in progress, we did what we could to earn a bit extra; and we did a lot of praying, planning, and making things for the new Carmel. Those of the Community who were good at joinery made tables and benches; others made clothing, sheets and other domestic linen. For a while I baked cakes and pies for sale, and another sister her delicious wholemeal loaves. These were very popular – I don't suppose we charged as much as we could have done for them. A friend took trays of these bakeries to the nearby village on Saturday mornings, and once they found out about it all the housewives would come along with plates and baskets to collect whatever they chose. The lady selling them for us quite enjoyed seeing the procession of customers hurrying off home carrying their bargains. One of the local pubs used to place a regular order. It all helped; but I think some of the sisters found it quite hard, as they munched their dry bread for breakfast whilst the mouth-watering aroma of fresh bakery and savoury pies wafted around the house from my first oven-load of the day!

Our own alterations were basically complete by then, but we kept the hens going for another year or two. People were also very kind, and we received gifts of money from well-wishers – often just little sums from pensioners and others of small means, but given with so much love that they meant more to us than if a very wealthy person had given much.

The work progressed rapidly once the foundations had been laid. The walls were made of pre-cast panels with a pebbled exterior, quite quick to assemble. As the winter came on, the builders managed to get the whole area roofed over so that the walls could begin to dry out. The site was fairly high up on the side of the hill, and bitterly cold winds swept through and around the building. These, it was hoped, would speed the drying. Perhaps they did; but it all remained very damp and cold for a long time. Once the roof was on, however, our Prioress – never one to waste time – arranged that we would go over from Thicket, a car-load at a time, and begin to decorate the rooms. She herself was an expert at painting and decorating and would be one of the party nearly every time, so that she could keep an eye on the work that was being done. She was Sister Mary, who at the time of the journey to York from Exmouth had planned all the details with such foresight. She had been elected Prioress in 1960.

I went on a couple of these expeditions, though I was not the world's best painter. I tended to paint the floor and myself almost as much as the ceilings and walls, but I was so keen to go that I think she put me in as an extra. Oh, it was so very, very cold – mid-January, no heating whatsoever in this newly-built shell, doors and windows all flung wide open to facilitate this mythical drying, and nothing hot to eat or drink! We took sandwiches for our mid-day meal, but we had no thermos flasks or kettle – in any case, there was as yet no electricity to heat anything. On one day the kind sisters at the Centre came up with a big jug of hot soup. I found this a life-saver; but the others who were with me seemed to think little of it – they just wanted to push on and get the scrubbing and painting done.

I managed to slip out into the surrounding woodland for a few moments at some point, just to see what it was all like. There wasn't time to go far, but I could get some idea of how it looked – wild, unkempt woodland and scrub, very different from the Thicket garden, but with a beauty of its own. It was January, so everything looked bare, but I could see wild raspberry canes, and various other recognisable shrubs. It was obviously a paradise for birds. I didn't know, then, that I was destined to spend the greater part of my life there; for at that stage the new foundation's Community had not yet been decided upon.

On one of those painting trips, Mother Prioress and two others went with several new cans of paint and were being driven happily along until they realised that they were being enveloped in a snow storm. There was already a lot of snow lying on the ground, but they had been told that the roads were clear, so they had sallied forth. Their driver got them as far as the village but saw that it would be impossible to get the car along the winding lane leading to Wood Hall – a drive of well over a mile. She wanted to turn back and make for home before the main roads became blocked. But Mother Prioress was not made like that. She and her helpers would walk, or wade, or crawl up that drive, carrying the heavy paint tins, come what may.

After some argument, it was obvious that she was perfectly serious about her decision; so the car turned and went away while the three snow-covered figures trudged their way along the already deep drifts in the lane. They slipped and slid and made slow progress, but every inch was a little further forward, and they just pushed on. When they had got about halfway, they thought they could hear an engine approaching. They looked round, hope surging up in their hearts. Sure enough, the postman's van was crawling along and catching up with them. He had a four-wheel drive, and was managing to advance.

The three bedraggled nuns looked up eagerly as he made his careful way along. He would have loved to let them all scramble into the van, but he had to tell them that post vans are forbidden to take passengers even in such circumstances. Regretfully, he drove on over the freezing snow, while they followed the little red van, clumping along in their snow-laden boots, clutching those paint-cans, the falling snow alighting on their eyelids and blurring their vision. On they went determinedly, trying to keep up their spirits: not much further now, surely? . . . On other visits, the drive had seemed so much shorter; but they had hitherto only travelled it by car.

After a while, the sound of an engine again broke the snowy silence. It was in front of them this time. Soon there came into view the postman's van again. He had managed to deliver the post to the Centre, and was trying to return to the village. He passed them, but scarcely had he done so than he began to be in difficulties, as the van tried to climb that last steep slope on the way down to Wood Hall. So our brave three nuns did what anyone else would have done in those arctic circumstances. They put down their paint-cans, turned round, and all helped to push the van up the hill until it could regain its grip at the top, and go chugging away.

There really wasn't much further to go for the sisters; the big house was already in sight. So they picked up their loads again and at last reached the shelter of a roof and human habitation. The staff saw their wet clothes – in those days we didn't wear coats or macs; but just went out in our habits, whatever the weather – and made them go into the kitchen to dry.

They gave them hot and, oh so welcome, tea. But true to form, Mother Prioress was in a hurry to go on up the hill to the shell that was the new Carmel. There was work to be done there and time was short. So very soon the three set off to go the little way up the hill, into the chilly building and straight to their painting.

It was February, and whether the electric lighting had been put in by then or whether they were still using oil lamps, I can't now recall – I was not one of the three. What I do know is that although she insisted on her two companions lying down for a rest at some point – there were no beds, just the bare floor – Mother Prioress herself went on painting for the rest of the day and all through the night. Sometime during the following afternoon our friend arrived with her car to take them home; the drive had by then been cleared sufficiently by some of the men at the Centre to make it navigable. She was amazed to see how the work had progressed. Nearly all the paint-cans were empty.

By March the painting was finished, and the house sparsely furnished with the essential needs for eight Sisters. March 19th, the Feast of St Joseph, was chosen for the opening day of the new Carmel. The list of names of the sisters who would constitute the little Community was sent to Rome – and Bridget was one of them.

chapter twenty-one

Wood Hall Carmel

It was on March 17th, St Patrick's Day, that the eight sisters set off from Thicket to begin the new Carmel. They ranged in age from late twenties to old Mother Mary of St John, who was eighty-seven. She had known what it was to begin new foundations, in her earlier years; and although by that time she was finding walking increasingly difficult she was very much on the spot mentally and could give good advice. Mother Mary of St John said of herself that she was coming to pray rather than to work. She didn't realise that one of her special gifts was to be such a lovely, supportive presence in any Community – something that was to be of great value over those first years. Eventually, she returned to Thicket, when she began to need more expert nursing. She lived to be well over ninety.

The sisters went by car, driven by kind friends. We waved good-bye to them, and God-speed; both they and we found the parting very hard. Although we were glad that a new Carmel was being founded, where prayer and praise would be going on all the time and where we knew the sisters would be happy, the cost to us all was very great. We who were left at Thicket felt utterly bereft. I remember going around the house, which now seemed so empty, later that day and seeing the pictures gone from each of the eight cells. We all have a small picture on the door of our cell, to indicate the occupant. Work had already been rearranged so that the daily chores were covered; but the sight of the choir stalls and refectory places with no one in them kept reminding us that we had lost more than a third of our Community.

The sisters who went on the foundation had so much to think about and do that they probably didn't feel the loss so acutely at first. They were busy getting the new house in order, lighting paraffin stoves in the rooms to try to warm them, preparing for the opening ceremony on the nineteenth, and generally getting their

165

bearings. The director and sisters from the Centre were kindness itself, and came to the door now and again to see if anything was needed that they could supply. They greatly appreciated the coming of the Carmel to Wood Hall. It added a whole new dimension to the work of the Centre – a 'praying presence'. Bishop Wheeler was overjoyed when he came to sing the first Mass on March 19th, the feast of St Joseph – a day we have kept as a very special anniversary ever since. So also was Father Paul White, who had encouraged us to make the foundation. Everything in the house was small, and cheap, or home-made; but it was a beginning. The sisters had come, the regular life of prayer had begun, and a new branch of the tree of Carmel had sprung forth and unfurled its leaves.

It was in June that we again had disturbing news from Ashcott. Mother had become very ill and Father was tottering around trying to nurse her. Again there was much heart-searching, but I soon realised that something had to be done, and done quickly. So this time it was I who made the long journey by coach from Yorkshire to Somerset. I filled a suitcase with all the things I thought might be useful or a treat for my parents – things like tins and jars of foodstuffs that were very heavy, so that I could scarcely lift the case. It would have been far more sensible to take some money to buy the things when I got there; but I didn't realise that, at the time. When I reached Cheltenham, where I had to change coaches, and was hauling this heavy load along, a young lad of about eleven ran up and offered to carry it for me. This was a huge relief – but I was so unused to the ways of travellers that I just thanked him very much and got into the new coach. It was only after we'd moved out of the station that I realised that the poor boy had carried my case in the hope of a tip, and most probably spent his free time earning his pocket-money like that. I felt miserable, but there was absolutely nothing to be done about it by then. I just hoped that the incident hadn't put him off nuns for the rest of his life. I have prayed for him so often since that day!

It was a beautiful sunny day, and the coach was travelling due south. It was nearly twenty years since I had been on a bus, but somehow I didn't feel at all strange. I looked out at the English countryside, noticing the place names and the features of the landscape. It was all new to me until we began to get into Wessex, and then a great feeling of familiarity and homecoming came over me. The grass seemed to become greener and brighter, and there were apple orchards with their trees bent over by the wind. Gloucestershire passed, then – yes, Somerset – the Mendips, with their often dramatic outcrops of rock and their patches of woodland. I was nearly home, after all those years. I had never thought I would see any of it again. I even had a glimpse of the sea at Weston-super-mare, because the coach called there before going on to Bridgwater. Although I was anxious about the state my dear parents might be in when I reached Ashcott, my heart was full of gratitude for this wholly unexpected happiness.

When we stopped at Bridgwater, there beside the road stood a great friend of the family from my childhood days, Mrs Bartlett. She had promised to meet me in her car and there she was, with her rosy apple cheeks, big smile, and the smart high-heeled shoes she always loved to wear when she was dressed up. I was amazed at how little she had altered in appearance over the almost twenty years since I had left home. She soon heaved that ridiculously heavy case into the back of her car, and before long we were speeding through the familiar villages, talking as we went. Until I heard her voice, I hadn't realised how much I had missed the Somerset way of speech. It sounded so musical – and so much more like American than I had ever noticed before. I suppose that many of the Pilgrim Fathers would have been Wessex men.

And so it was that in the golden sunlight of a late afternoon in June that I arrived back in Ashcott. We drove up the lane to the big back gate. It opened as if by magic and out bounded a handsome young man, well over six foot tall, who gathered me into his arms for a quick hug and then picked up that hefty suitcase as if it had been a handbag. It was Julian. He had dashed home when he heard how ill Mother was and had arrived not long before me. I think he had hitch-hiked – his usual mode of transport at that time.

Up the stone-flagged courtyard – oh, so well remembered! – I walked, following him into the hall, which looked dim after the bright sunlight outside. There it was, just as it had always been, the heavy oak beam supporting the ceiling and upstairs rooms, the twisty stairs, the coats hanging on a row of pegs against the wall. What used to be the jam-cupboard, where the mice used to get into any pots not covered with a piece of wood, had been opened up, and made into the attractive alcove it must originally have been. Otherwise, little had changed.

My mind was almost in a daze, and yet in a sense ultra-perceptive, as I went into the living-room. A white-haired man was seated in the big chair by the empty fire-place. He didn't at that moment attempt to rise – that would have been too lengthy a process for this most precious encounter. I bent over him and gave my father a kiss and a big hug.

'I have dreamed so often that you came home', he said, 'but it's never been true before'.

I went across the hall to the other room. They had been using this as a bedroom since he had broken his hip. Neither of them could really manage the stairs any more. Mother lay there in bed, looking worn and grey, and was obviously very poorly. She had had a lot of pain. Father had spent hours just sitting on the side of her bed, holding her hand. They were still so much in love.

Soon I was bustling around in the kitchen, getting out the things I had brought with me, and making a meal for us all. Julian was a great help, telling me where everything was. I saw that he really had changed very little in character from the four-year-old I had left behind when I entered Carmel. Mother had been visited by the doctor earlier in the day, and had pills of various kinds that she was supposed to be taking. Both she and Father didn't believe in taking pills. 'Let's have blue ones today!' Father would say brightly. She understood about the insulin – but even with that I was never too happy about the way she did it. She used the same 'clean water' to rinse the syringe until it had a green edge all around the top. Yet she managed to do the injection for well over twenty years – perhaps hers was a charmed life!

In a few days there was a marked improvement in Mother's condition, and Bou rang up to say she was coming over from Street with the children. This was normally the best of tonics for the grandparents, but because of Mother's illness they had feared that the noise and exuberance of children would have been inadvisable. It was the day the bread-man called – not the baker with his own freshly-baked wares of my childhood, but a van that brought round mass-produced loaves and some cakes and pastries. Father insisted I bought plenty of these buns and some sausage rolls for the children – 'Grandpa's party', he called it. I discovered that he always did this if he knew they were coming; and no doubt the children had no difficulty in emptying the plates.

That was another very poignant day for me. I had not seen Bou since our early days at Thicket, before she was married, and now she had an already large family. Her husband, David, I hadn't seen since he was a school-boy. They came in an elderly car, and spilled out into the paddock, the two boys dashing straight off on some game. They were about eight and ten years old. Then came two fairy-like figures with long silky hair, one of them so like Bou at that age that I could hardly believe my eyes. Melinda and Julia looked at me shyly, as if I had dropped from another planet; I suppose I did look a rarity in my brown habit, although they were accustomed to seeing nuns in church and at school. Then came Edmund, the baby, just asserting himself in his new rôle as a toddler; he was captivating, with his wise, dark eyes and thoughtful expression as he calmly summed me up.

And there was my dear Bou. We just wanted to look at one another for the first few moments, as time stood still and the years slipped away. We had been together so often in that paddock in our childhood and growing days, and now her children were enjoying the same pleasures, in the same place.

Her relief at my coming was beyond words. She had been torn apart with Mother so ill yet her loyalties to her husband and children keeping her from being able to help. It was an agony that both she and I were to have to live through, over the coming years, quite often – the others, too – as our parents became progressively more frail and in need of help. Yet in their way they were a determined and obstinate couple – they always felt sure that they could manage and were 'perfectly all right'. Father was eighteen years older than Mother, but hers was a less robust constitution; so there were times, like this one, when they just had to give in. In one way it was hard to see them both so frail and failing, yet all the same we felt proud of their courage and tenacity. They both still had that wonderful gift of being able to enjoy life. A flower, a bud on a treasured plant, a sunset, a goldfinch on a thistle – any one of the daily wonders surrounding them filled them with delight and joy. Even things read in the paper, or a book, they would share with happy zest – 'Listen to this, Mum', Father would say, as he sat in his chair, glasses perched precariously – because one arm of them was replaced by a piece of twisted wire – and then he'd read out some funny anecdote for her pleasure.

Bou and I had so much to discuss and to remember; and as we still do whenever we get the opportunity to speak together on the phone, we found ourselves full of gratitude for our parents, our home, and all that we had received from our upbringing. We recalled what Father had said to us so often in days gone by – 'Write two words over your bed: Patience and Courage', and his other recommendation: 'Press on with courage and fortitude' – I think that one was a legacy of his war years. He was certainly living out his own advice before our eyes.

On another occasion Simon came over, too, with his wife and two children. So my errand of mercy had its very happy side in that I was able to see my family again and meet for the first time all my little nieces and nephews. Once Mother began to improve I was able to appreciate these bonuses better, though at the same time I couldn't forget that my Community back in Carmel were doing my jobs for me, and longing for me to come back. Someone said to me recently, and I've found it so true, that the stupendous and the trivial are inextricably intertwined in our lives. Even in the greatest moments and experiences one part of us is worrying over some tiny detail – whether we left enough water in the kettle, or if we'd remembered to switch something off. Maybe part of the lesson I was trying to learn from my parents now was the ability they had of enjoying life to the full, and not worrying about something that at that moment they could do nothing about; in other words, to live in the present moment, and make the best use of it.

The village had already changed a good deal over the almost twenty years that I had been away. When I left there were lots of small orchards, like our own, behind farms and in between the houses. These had now almost all disappeared and been replaced by clusters of bungalows, each with its brightly-coloured and well tended garden. The view from the front rooms in our house was quite different. The cow-byre and midden that had been in the foreground had gone, and a cottage now stood in its place, with a gold-fish pond and pretty shrubs. The couple living in it had been children when I last saw them – I felt a bit like Rip van Winkle! Further down the lane, the huge chestnut tree and the beech, both of which had been landmarks in the village, had also gone. Bungalows had grown up on that land, too. The occupants had planted other, smaller trees – laburnums, red mays and various flowering shrubs – and while I was feeling sad at the loss of the big trees, Father was telling me of the beauty of those new ones, and the colourful sight they made as he looked from his window. He was so remarkably young at heart still, and I blessed him for it.

Already the village was home to a much larger population; in fact, it was fast becoming a dormitory village. Gone were the days when everyone knew everyone, and a stranger was an object of interest and discussion. Yet a good deal of it still remained the same – I could still see Pedwell Hill from the bedroom windows, and had only to walk to the top of the nearby lane to be able to look across to Glastonbury Tor. One quite striking change, though, that I noticed was that it seemed everyone now had a bathroom, flush toilet, car (or more than one), telephone, refrigerator, and a television. Within a few more years these were to be joined by a deep-freeze and a video. In the gardens motor mowers and power tools had appeared. So a lot of things that had been non-existent in village homes had now become basic necessities. My parents had never had a car, and would never have been able to afford a telephone or television. It was one of their children who insisted that they had a phone put in as they became more frail, and in fact had it installed for them. Father was perfectly certain that they did *not* need it and eyed it with disgust at first. But very soon it became a great joy to him, as he realised he could talk to any of his children in their own homes, and that it really was a very good idea for house-bound people.

Their television was also given to them by Father's brother, Harry, and his wife, Lily. They kindly kept up the payments of the rental and licence until they died.

Several things, however, had virtually disappeared from the home scene, the most noticeable one being the hearth. All down the centuries, and during my own growing years, the words 'home and hearth' were very closely connected, hearth meaning and being the very centre, the heart-beat of home. However poor the home, even the veritable hovel that many families lived in, the parents and often small children gathered fuel to make a fire. Food was cooked on it, and in the cold winter evenings everyone gathered round the last embers for warmth and a glimmer of light. In the homes of the better-off the fire would be in the living-room, and everyone would be gathered there. Children would be doing their homework, or reading, or playing games or music. Fathers would be reading the paper, or a book; mothers often making or mending garments, grannies knitting. I felt sorry, and rather apprehensive, when I saw that this symbol of home, family and security had almost gone. The danger, to my eyes, was fragmentation.

Until recently, the ability of a man and woman to make and control fire was a sign of civilization. Today there are adults leaving universities who have no idea of how to light a fire. It is no longer a basic skill. Maybe it's just something they will never need to know. New skills have replaced the very down-to-earth, elemental expertise of former ages. Life was tougher, but simpler.

I stayed at Ashcott for three weeks, by which time Mother was on her feet again, frail but determined. It was hard to leave them – almost harder than when I'd first left home, because they were now so needy. But we were all three as brave as we could manage; and they did in fact cope for some time before the next real illness. Meanwhile I received a most loving welcome back at Carmel – my other family.

chapter twenty-two

Creating a garden

During the following months there were some changes made in the Community at Wood Hall. Bridget was not at all well there, so she came back to Thicket. Later one of the others had a fall and broke her arm and she too returned. Each of these was replaced by another sister. One found the life in a new, pioneering situation difficult to cope with. For various reasons the new Community went through a time of rearrangement; and so therefore did we. This had been anticipated – it would have been impossible to judge beforehand exactly who was really needed at Thicket, and who would be most suited to the new task of making the foundation.

It was lovely for me to have Bridget back. She soon regained her health and youthful bloom. The Prioress was glad to have her at Thicket again, for she was gifted in many ways and was a helper for her. She stayed on, and has been at Thicket ever since.

It was not until early next May, just over a year after the new house was founded, that our Prioress asked me if I would be willing to go to Wood Hall. Somehow it was all so simple. I loved Thicket, and the sisters there, and the beautiful garden; yet when the call came I knew I was quite ready to pack my very few belongings and set off on the next stage of my journey. We had a little party in the kitchen – scene of so many of my labours! – and everyone gave me helpful suggestions and ideas for what to do and take. By this time we had become more accustomed to the idea of sisters going and coming back, so we made jokes about how long it would be before I returned. This blunted the sharp edge of the parting, or at least helped to obscure it from our immediate view.

Events moved swiftly, and before the end of May a friend's car was at the door, and my little box of belongings was being put into the boot. Most of my luggage consisted of plants I had dug up from the garden, because I knew the Wood Hall garden was as yet just a rough, stony hillside. This caused some merriment among my Community – 'Burnham Wood coming to Dunsinane' – and 'She's taking half the garden'. 'How will the driver see the way through all those leaves?' and other comments. But I wasn't going to leave any behind, after having gone to the trouble of digging them up.

A last goodbye, and then I was speeding through the Yorkshire villages towards Wetherby. The couple who were driving me were very kind, and managed to make everything seem as normal as possible – as if I were just out for the day. They chatted amicably, and pointed out various places of interest as we passed. It was not a long drive, less than an hour; so soon we were on the bumpy lane up to Wood Hall. I had last seen it on one of my painting and scrubbing expeditions, when snow covered the surrounding fields, and the trees and hedges were bare. Now all was green with that first lovely brightness of spring, the new leaves freshly unfurled, and the verges full of wild flowers.

When we reached the new little Carmel, and I saw its bare pebble-dash frontage, I realised how different it was all going to be externally from Thicket, with its spacious rooms and solid walls. But I knew that the inner spirit would be just the same, and that it would still be home. Before we had pulled up at the door – there wasn't even a porch in those early days! – it was thrown open, and two of the sisters came hurrying out to meet me. We quickly unloaded the car, while my kind friends were given some tea. I wanted to get my plants into a sheltered corner until I could put them into the ground.

Then I had a great welcome from the rest of the little Community. It was indeed home from home in that these were all part of our original group at Thicket; I knew them all so well, as they did me. I was shown my new cell, the choir, the refectory – all very small and poor after Thicket, but adequate for the time being, while we were so few. The kitchen was unbelievably tiny, with a two-burner paraffin stove for all the cooking. Sister Mary Bernard had mastered its ways, and could make the bread and cakes in its little oven. Two loaves and a tray of brown bread-buns were cooling on a rack as I went in to look around.

And there was dear old Mother Mary of St John, coming along

with her staff. She didn't want a walking stick, because she said it would make her bend over; she liked a tall staff instead. I had cut it for her while she was still at Thicket, from a young ash sapling. She was so pleased to see me. After all, she'd been my Prioress for most of my time as a nun, and my novice-mistress as well during my years of initial training. She was to be a support to me now, as I began this new phase of my life; and I was soon appointed to help her in everyday things where she needed someone at hand, now that she was old and infirm.

Although the same horarium was followed as at Thicket, we had to be far more flexible and ready to change things round at short notice. Because we shared the chapel with the Ecumenical Centre, our main church service of the day, Mass, might be at any hour from early morning to mid-day – occasionally even in the afternoon or evening. We had to fit in with whatever group of people happened to be staying at the Centre on that day. This could be quite difficult at times, particularly if we didn't know beforehand exactly when it would be. There was bread to be put to rise – we always made our own, then – and the printing press to ink up. It was no joke to get everything ready for printing and then have to break off for an hour, with the ink left to get sticky on the rollers. The printing was our livelihood.

The reverse side of that particular coin was that very often some of the best speakers of the time were at the Centre giving lectures or courses in the chapel, and we were able to be present and to profit from the talks. In that way we made friends who still keep in touch today.

The garden was simply a wide sweep of hillside, full of stones. There were just a few inches of stony soil over solid rock, covered with wild grass and brambles. Everyone said we'd never be able to grow anything on it. Yet when they had been at Wood Hall for just a year, the sisters had started a vegetable-patch, and some beans and cabbages were already looking promising. The far side of the hill was a tangle of natural woodland, mainly ash, sycamore and wych-elm, with an understorey of spindle trees and hawthorn. It was a long time before we were able really to explore it and discover some of its secrets.

Our main concern was to clear the area near the house and on the sunny side of the hill, and to plant trees, shrubs and an orchard, as well as the vegetable patch. All around the house was as it had been left by the bulldozer that had levelled the land for the building. There were jagged pieces of broken rock lying everywhere; and a steep bank of debris faced the windows immediately outside the cells. It was certainly a challenging site!

Not many of us were strong enough for garden work; and even those who were had to help with indoor tasks as well, so we could not spend as much time out of doors as we would have liked – in fact, gardening time had perforce to come fairly far down the list of daily priorities. But what time we could find, even sometimes a bare five minutes, we would use, so that very gradually, almost imperceptibly, a transformation began to take place.

Sometimes a relation or friend sent a gift of cash to 'get something for the garden', and I would pore over gardening books and catalogues so as to be able to choose the most suitable plants and shrubs for such inhospitable conditions. The hillside was high up and very windswept, which made it bleak and wintry even when the surrounding lower-lying villages had begun to show signs of spring.

No one looking at the garden today could ever imagine what it was like. There are lawns full of daisies in summer, cowslips in springtime; shrubs and flowering trees give colour and interest all the year round. The rough, rocky bank is clothed with plants and shrubs – and many weeds too, or rather, wild plants! There is an orchard that yields enough fruit to keep the community in apples for the best part of the year, and some over to give to anyone who comes. Then, further along the hillside, a large and productive vegetable garden, with greenhouses and rows of soft fruit, gives ample evidence of the value of perseverance.

It has all been done step by step, almost inch by inch. Each autumn we bought, or had given us, one or two fruit trees, every one of which could only be planted by digging the hole first with a pickaxe, cutting into rock, then filling the cavity with compost. Nothing was wasted; everything was composted, because this thin layer of soil dries out very quickly in summer, so anything that will make a mulch is eagerly sought after. I'd long known that where there is little or no soil, cultivation will eventually make some; there were times when it was hard for us to believe this, but in the end we saw that it was in fact true.

Five hundred years ago the original Thicket Priory was one of many thriving monasteries in Yorkshire, some of which were for men and for women. They were centres of prayer, learning and expertise, and helped to create the Yorkshire we know today, with its sheep-grazing and cultivated fields. Few people were aware, as we struggled to get the new little foundation on its feet, that a new Yorkshire monastery was springing up in this quiet place near Wetherby. The ones who did know were overjoyed, and deeply appreciative. It is to their encouragement and assistance, as much as to the tenacity and courage of the small founding group of sisters, that we owe our being here today.

The monks and nuns of those olden days must have struggled with the same problems that beset us. They too had to hack their way through rocks, and slash at brambles with hand-tools similiar to the ones we had. We never had anyone to help in the garden – or for that matter in the house either. We did all our own decorating, joinery – Sister Catherine made some wonderful cupboards and shelving – and repairs of all kinds, as well as making our clothes, and building retaining walls and steps. Only for electrical or plumbing problems that were really beyond our competence were we obliged to get help from outside. We could not have afforded to pay anyone – it was as simple as that. We had no power tools, just a few basic and trusty things such as the pickaxe, spade, fork, hammer and saw – in fact, the very same equipment that those monks and nuns of old would have used – indeed, everyone, until the last comparatively few years.

Those first years were not easy. There were difficulties of all kinds, some of them having no simple solution. At one point the Prioress and her council at Thicket began to fear that it had all been a big mistake, and that we should have waited longer before making the foundation. They had heard about the services held in the chapel for the groups of young people (and some not so young!) who came to the courses at the Centre, bringing their guitars and drums, flutes and clarinets plus any other available instruments, to accompany their enthusiastic singing. Thicket feared that this might impinge on the silence and solitude that is so much a part of our Carmelite life. Had they been present themselves at these services they would have realised at once the great faith of the participants, and the spirit of prayer and praise that was so evident to us. When one has only hearsay to go on, everything becomes distorted. So there was a lot of suffering both here and at Thicket over this and similiar issues. It was all part of the growing pains of a new foundation. St Teresa used to say that if everything went too easily when she made her foundations it was not a good sign! Certainly we didn't have it easy here. Yet there were many consolations, and deep within us a peace and tranquillity as we all felt that 'all shall be well and all manner of thing shall be well' as Julian of Norwich said; so we resolutely went quietly on, praying and working.

It was a very happy day for us all when our first postulant asked to join the Community. It must have been a great step in faith for her, considering the smallness and poverty of the house. Nevertheless she came, and she stayed. It was the beginning of January when she arrived, and very cold – one of the funny anecdotes she enjoys recounting of her early days here was how she used to put her anorak on in bed in the effort to get warm enough to sleep! She brought with her anything she felt might be of use to us when she sold her home and belongings; it was all put to good use around the house, and some is still going strong to this day.

Those years were a testing time and a growing time for all Religious Orders and Congregations, as the new approaches of the Second Vatican Council slowly opened up windows and doors of thought. Attitudes began to change, emphases shifted – when you have lived as long as I have it is quite astonishing to see just how radically people's ways of looking at life, the Church, even themselves, have altered in one lifetime. The most important things haven't changed, of course, nor can they. Reality and truth will always remain. But the way we see things, and the expectations we cherish differ from generation to generation, and even from person to person. I like to think that we see more clearly today; but no doubt people have thought the same since creation began.

Certainly for us in Carmel a few welcome changes came about in some areas of our lives, just as they did in the world around us. Record players and cassettes began to appear, so that those of us who had loved instrumental music were able to enjoy it again on occasion. The heavy iron grilles, through which we used to see our visitors, were removed. Lighter habits were made for the summer-time, and – wonder of wonders! – tea and coffee made their way into everyday life. The important things remained, as we hope they always will – prayer, silence, community life. It was the outer trappings of the life that were, and are, being updated.

In order for the monastery to be fully recognised and ratified, we had to have sufficient room for a minimum of thirteen sisters, so we needed to build on more cells and enlarge the tiny kitchen and refectory. It all seemed a daunting task, because our printing work was barely keeping us afloat financially. But again, people helped, and God blessed our efforts. We began to build, even though at the time we hadn't enough money to pay the first instalment of the builder's bills; but when the day came for the bill to arrive there was just enough in the bank to cover it. So it went on, until the cells were completed; it was quite miraculous, and we saw it in that light. Gifts of money came, or gifts in kind, when our earnings were not sufficient.

One very wonderful present was given to us by the mother of one of the sisters. She had seen the little oil-stove in the kitchen. 'An army marches on its stomach', she quoted; and she gave us our Aga cooker, which has been at the heart of the home ever since. We had had an Aga at Thicket, so I already loved cooking with one – maybe it was not such a far cry from the tiny range we had at home.

Before long another postulant joined us, bringing joy to us all. Things were still fairly primitive – the new cells were just ready, but so much remained to be done. It was when she was a Novice that we first ventured into keeping goats. People had told us that our land was the very place for goats; there was lots for them to eat so their upkeep would cost little. In fact, they would help to tidy up the garden and woods; and we'd have plenty of milk, which would be good for everyone.

The goats duly arrived, round about Sister Catherine's Silver Jubilee, so they were called Silver and Jubilee. Both were British Saanens, but very different in character. Silver was a thoroughbred, perfect in all her points, and was accompanied by the most endearing little kid, which we called Goldberry after one of Tolkien's characters; but she was rather obtuse. Jubilee was just the opposite, with her rough coat and oddly-shaped figure. Her job before coming to us was to run on the hills with the flocks of sheep, and act as foster-mother to any orphaned lambs.

Unlike the handsome but somewhat dim-witted Silver, she was highly intelligent and great fun to be with. She arrived first, so our attempts at milking began with her. It was Sister Melanie who was to care for the goats, although she had grown up in the city, and had never milked anything before. She loved animals, so we knew that she would do the job well. In the book about goat-keeping, it said that if the goat could be persuaded to stand on a bench the operation would be much easier for the milker, as goats are quite low on the ground.

Goats enjoy climbing, so it was no problem to get her to stand on the garden bench; and Melanie began to milk. However, no milk came despite helpful hints being read out by other sisters. Goats are sociable animals and like to be talked to. Sister Patricia spoke gently to Jubilee, who replied with a polite 'Maa...a', revealing as she opened her mouth the heads of my purple lupins, on which she had been browsing to my chagrin a few minutes before. 'It says here: "the goat should feel relaxed and comfortable at milking times"', Patricia read out. 'Relax Jubilee', she urged. Whereupon Jubilee promptly sat down, so that was the end of the first attempt at milking.

We really enjoyed goat-husbandry. They lived at first in a small hut in the garden which was normally used as a hermitage for prayer. Subsequently we built a real house for them, with breeze-blocks, containing everything a goat would wish for, and providing storage space for their winter feed. We worked together on this for some time, and when it was complete we had a house-warming. We lit a bonfire outside in which to roast potatoes, and had our dinner up there – it was all freshly white-washed, and had not yet been lived in by the future occupants.

Both the goats and little Goldberry greatly enjoyed the day. They really love human company. Next day they couldn't understand why we weren't going to do it again, and kept calling for us all day!

Unfortunately as time went on, the goats discovered the vegetable garden. Although this was surrounded by three-foot wire netting to keep the woodland rabbits out, the rows of tender young greens and lettuces soon had them bounding over. Goats and vegetables simply cannot live on the same patch.

Sadly we had to sell the goats; but the director of the Centre bought a cow for us as a gift in honour of his own Silver Jubilee of Ordination. She, too, was therefore called Jubilee.

Wood Hall Carmel

The Community Room at Wood Hall

chapter twenty-three

The Lore of the Land

Jubilee was a gentle Jersey cow, very beautiful with her big brown-navy eyes and curly top-knot. Though small, she seemed quite large to us after milking the goats. She settled in straight away, living in the goat house, suitably adapted for her. Jubilee seemed to know instinctively what she should do as a monastic cow, and became part of the family very quickly. She too loved company, and would watch the people coming up to the chapel with great interest.

I was cook at the time, and used to make butter and cheese with her rich Jersey milk, as indeed I had with the goats' milk. The butter was usually successful, but the cheese varied considerably. Once it looked about to explode so we had to bury it! Another time we were very proud of it and gave some to a monk who was giving us talks, to take home to his community. We never heard a word about it from them and trust that they all lived to enjoy it!

We had an electric fence to divide the field into three parts, so that Jubilee could graze one part while another was growing for hay for her winter feed. A farmer cut the hay for us, and we then did all the rest ourselves by hand, tossing and raking it, and taking it in barrow-loads to near her shed where we built it into a rick. Hay-baling hadn't yet become the norm. It was hard work, but we pulled together and made a creditable little rick.

As with the goats, we had plenty of entertaining experiences while caring for the cow, and for her calf later on – as when Sister Melanie had to fill in the forms required as part of keeping dairy cows: Name of owner. Name of chief herdsman. Number of cows in herd – answer: one!

We had Jubilee for a couple of years. She gave birth to a beautiful calf which we named Petra, and later on sold to a local farmer. It was when she had her second calf that she became ill. The birth had been quite normal, with our vet in attendance, and a few of us spending part of the night up there in her shed with her.

Next morning she was lying down, which was very unusual. We called the vet again, and sadly he diagnosed milk-fever. He did what he could, but was unable to save our lovely cow. She died with her head on my lap, as I sat on the straw.

We were all distressed, and there were unashamed tears on many faces. To see the knacker-man come with his truck to collect her was cruel. There was, too, the problem of the bonny little bull-calf waiting to be fed – and no mother. Sister Melanie rang a good friend who lived in Lancashire for advice. It was a long way off, but this kind man got straight into his car and drove over. He was a farmer and had a foster mother ready for little Hubert, so he took him home.

Knowing we were all upset, he had thoughtfully brought three baby goslings with him. 'Try to rear these', he said. 'They'll help you to take your minds off Jubilee'. They were tiny balls of greeny-yellow fluff. He explained that goslings are never easy to rear, but if we managed to keep one out of the three we would be doing well. He had brought a bag of food for them, for the first week or two; after they'd finished that, they would be ready to live on grass, which was their staple diet.

At Thicket we'd had much experience in rearing chicks. Sister Catherine was put in charge of the three helpless little creatures, and I helped with any maintenance they required. You might wonder what that entailed, but I assure you it was a surprising amount! First, we had to make a pen for them – wooden sides, netting top, and a little fox-proof shelter at the back for the night-time.

As all three goslings grew at an astonishing rate, we soon had to build bigger quarters for them, allowing them to roam the orchard during the day. They kept the grass down so well around the baby apple trees that it was like a bowling green. Never before nor since has it looked like that!

They loved music, and when people were singing in the chapel they listened with ecstatic attention, their long white necks stretched upward, heads a little to one side. They got to know Sister Catherine's voice well, because she was usually the one who fed them. One hot summer's day she had the window wide open in her office – she was Prioress at the time – and when the phone rang she stood by the window to answer it. The three geese heard her voice as she talked on the phone and thought she must be calling them. They came hurtling down from the orchard, half running and half flying, and landed hopefully outside her window.

As Christmas came, the full-grown geese inevitably went and we didn't keep livestock any more, apart from a couple of useful cats. We reverted to the 'paper cow' – buying dried milk in a large paper sack for most uses, and a few bottles of fresh milk for tea and coffee, and for visitors. It worked out quite reasonably, and was less demanding of our time and energy. Around that time we took up the making of eucharistic wafers for churches, to supplement what we earned by our printing. This is fairly simple work, in which several of the sisters can share; and the demand is steady. So our time was taken up with getting this under way.

Early in the 1980s we had the sad experience of losing all the beautiful wych-elms that had been a great feature of our woodland. Dutch elm disease struck, as it did all over the country, and we had to have every one felled. Some were huge, majestic trees that must have taken many years to attain so great a height and girth. Chain-saws roared and screamed throughout the woods, tractors ploughed through the under-growth, until it all looked like a battlefield. When I heard the dull, cruel crump of those giant trees crashing to the ground I used to bow my head in silent pain for a minute or two.

Yet, if left unfelled, the elms would have died and blown down eventually, spreading the disease. It was explained to me that by felling them before they had begun to rot the timber would be saved, and put to good use. But I still found it a sad experience. Most of our trees were cut up on the site into pit-props, and were to be used in a coal-mine quite far under the North Sea. The better trees were carted away on long trailers.

When the man from the Forestry Commission was looking over the trees, he and I were walking along one of the woodland paths when he noticed a stripped sapling.

'I see you have deer', he said.

'Oh no', I replied confidently. 'But we used to keep goats'.

He looked more closely at the sapling. 'But this is freshly done', he maintained.

'No, we don't have deer. We have foxes and badgers, but not deer', I answered with complete assurance.

It was not long afterwards that Sister Rose was working in the woods and watched three graceful roe-deer bounding along the woodland ride. As often, I was wrong. Deer had indeed moved into the area, and browsed in our own and the surrounding woods and fields. They have been part of our fauna ever since, and never fail to give delight when we suddenly see them. They even come close to the house at times, and from the windows we have watched them feeding.

For a while after the trees had gone whole areas of the woods looked clear and bare; but with the sunlight now flooding the once shaded floor that had worn a carpet of dog's mercury and twayblades, all became inexorably an impenetrable mass of brambles. We are still working on the clearing and replanting process. Many ash and sycamore saplings came up without our aid; but there has been a lot to do as we help them through their younger stages. We love our woodlands, and the wild-life they shelter. I have had magical moments meeting foxes, deer, squirrels, hares – plenty of rabbits, too, but we are not quite so fond of these because of their skill at getting into the vegetable garden.

I could tell you many adventures concerning the badgers, including the saga of finding one of their setts had been tampered with, and subsequently catching the men digging there in broad daylight. The headline in a local paper ran: 'Men digging badger sett caught in act by Nun'. We were able to smile when we saw that, but in fact it was a very distressing experience. We had fondly imagined that the badgers were safe on our property; we knew only too well the cruelty the poor creatures undergo when they are caught. Now we realised that they were as vulnerable here as anywhere else – and so, for that matter, were we.

Also of interest is our success with apple trees grown from pips. In our early days here, old Sister Raphael used to save the pips from her apples in the refectory – we would see her fumbling in her pocket during the meal and bringing out a little piece of paper. She would carefully wrap the pips from her apple in this, and put it aside with an air of quiet satisfaction. Later on the pips were planted in pots of soil; then, as the weeks went by, it was her delight to see tiny seedlings emerge. It was a hobby she had, being a good gardener in her way, though somewhat unorthodox.

I like to think that I too have had a share in those trees, because if she forgot to water them for a spell I would give them a splosh as I passed by them; as they grew larger it was I who planted them in a nursery bed, and kept an eye on their welfare. Ultimately I planted them in the orchard. As the years passed, they began to bear fruit. A few were not very exciting – small and not much bigger than crab-apples, so we scrapped them. But the majority produced splendid apples - each, of course, a brand new variety. Raphael saw the first two fruit before she died in 1982. Since then the others have fruited, and so we are the proud possessors of some unique apples. One is a very early eater, another an early and large cooker which becomes an eater as it ripens. Then there are some mid-season varieties, and perhaps the most useful of all two very late keepers – this year we used the last of them in June. One day these trees may be worth propagating.

All down the years we have steadfastly refused to use poisonous weedkillers, sprays, or any other chemical substances that could endanger our little patch of countryside. Sometimes it's hard to resist the temptation to get rid of the weeds the easy way, but we prefer to know that our vegetables, fruit and flowers are free from poisons. It means we get lots of greenfly, caterpillars and slugs – but as we also love the wild birds we feel we are providing a good habitat for them, and for all the other wild-life around. And even when the slugs have done their bit, the pigeons theirs, and all the other hazards of a gardener's life have had their share, we still manage to produce good food for the Community. After all, it isn't meant to be a show garden, though it is certainly an interesting one. The latest problem is deer eating the spinach, for which they have a weakness. No wonder they look so healthy!

187

Mother in her sixties

chapter twenty-four

The old Soldier

It was in the spring of 1977 that a phone message came from Ashcott to say that Father was very poorly, and Mother had had a fall and hurt her leg. They were in sore straits. I was cook at the time, and was busily kneading dough for the making of some fancy bread-buns, for it was Easter Eve, and the morrow would be a festive day. Our Prioress came into the kitchen to tell me of the call, and I saw at once that I would have to go and help them, since none of the others could do so.

I rubbed the flour off my hands on my apron, and ran upstairs to put a few oddments I might need into a bag. Meanwhile the other sisters were making the necessary travel arrangements. In an incredibly short time I was sitting in a train, speeding down the length of England to Bridgwater, where Julian was to meet me and drive me to Ashcott.

It was all like a dream, yet with heavy foreboding in it. The last time I had gone home both parents had got well again quite soon, and on another occasion when Bridget had gone she, too, had managed to get them back onto their feet again, even though they were not really in a fit condition to be living on their own and looking after themselves. Somehow they managed; and the local doctor kept her eye on them once a week.

By the time we reached Bridgwater it was much later than scheduled, and Julian was wondering what could have happened. He had his wife and baby son with him in the car. They had been with our parents during the afternoon as it was Saturday, and he was not working. They felt all would be well once I got there – someone to give them the care they needed at that difficult time. Mother's leg was not broken, but badly bruised and grazed, and she could only walk with difficulty.

We were soon in the car, and Julian put me in the picture as we drove along. We dropped Judy and the baby at their cottage in

Stawell, and sped on to Ashcott through those familiar villages. He had bought fish and chips to take home, so that there would be some supper for us all. 'Maybe Dad will perk up when he knows it's fish and chips', Julian said brightly.

When we reached the old house, Julian went in a little ahead of me. His younger ears had caught something that mine had missed. It was Mother's voice, talking. In a second he grasped what had happened. I followed him into my parents' room. Mother put down the phone. Father was sitting in his accustomed chair, upright, dignified, his hand on his knee; but his brave spirit had slipped away.

I went over and kissed his forehead. It was cold. 'Is it certain, Mar?' Julian asked, a glimmer of hope lingering yet in his eyes. 'Yes, I think it is', I said softly. Then I put my hand on his knee, and my own hope gave a tiny flicker. 'His knee is still warm!' Perhaps . . . then I realised that the electric fire was on beside him, turned low.

My heart had sunk again. 'It's the warmth from the fire'. I put my hands on his shoulders, strong square shoulders that had carried me often enough, long ago. I saw there was still some of the bread-dough around my nails – I hadn't had a proper wash since I had kneaded my buns on the kitchen table at Wood Hall.

Mother had realised not long before our arrival that he was no longer breathing. She had been waiting anxiously for me to come. It was getting so much later than I had been expected. Hardly knowing what she was doing, yet guided by that same sure instinct of wisdom that had helped her through so many difficult moments in the past, she had picked up the phone and rung Julian's cottage, hoping that he and I had at least got as far as that, and wanting us so much. It must have been the very moment that we had dropped Judy and the baby off, because she found the phone ringing when she opened her door, and hastened to answer it.

'I think something terrible has happened'. Mother's voice was enough without the words. Judy then did a very sensible thing. 'Just keep talking to me, Mum', she said. 'It doesn't matter what you say. Say anything – just keep talking. Ju and Marie will be with you any moment'.

So that was what Mother was doing when we came into the house. She was very brave. As yet her grief had not fully taken hold of her. She and I went into the other room, while Julian rang the doctor and undertaker. In moments like this, God gives a strength we could never have found in ourselves. I knew Mother ought to be having some food, because she was a diabetic on insulin, and had been under great strain. I remembered the fish and chips – always a celebration meal for her, as for Father. We warmed them up, and she managed to eat a little; so that was one of my worries eased.

The doctor had been at the house earlier in the day, but hadn't guessed how near the end Father was. He had just slipped away. Like the old soldiers in the song he used to sing, he had 'faded away'. It always used to upset Mother when he sang that song, in his lovely tenor voice, pausing on the top note.

Throughout her married life Mother had known that in all probability he would go before her, as he was eighteen years her senior. But he had been doing so well, and at eighty-six had still been as mentally alert as ever – the very evening before, he had been carrying on a deeply involved discussion with Julian. It had looked possible that they would reach their golden wedding, which was only a matter of months away. But we are never prepared for what we dread, and it is as well. When the moment comes it is time enough to bear it, without having tried to anticipate its pain.

We rang the rest of the family – or rather, Julian did, while I stayed with Mother. We did ordinary things, like feeding the cat and bird, and arranging for the night – she couldn't walk very well with her damaged leg. I fixed the bandage, trying to make it more comfortable. Somehow caring for the lesser wound distracted our minds from the great one. Julian carried her bed on his back up the twisty stairs, and put it beside the one I was to sleep in. I ran up to see if he needed help. He didn't need it with the bed, but both he and I needed to be alone together for a few moments. We let our tears flow, and held each other very close. 'He's been more ill than that so often', he said, 'but he's always been able to pull through'. I don't remember my answer, if there was one. We dried our faces and went back downstairs. I had a kind of fear that once she saw our tears Mother's would begin, and I couldn't imagine how they would ever end. But I misjudged her courage. She was an example to us both. Then Julian went home to his cottage and family, and we went up to bed.

Very early next morning Julian's car came back up the road. Neither he nor we had been able to sleep. Later on Bou and her husband came, and in the afternoon Simon. It was Easter Sunday, the day of Resurrection – surely the most fitting day of the whole year to be thinking in terms of new life and the resurrection of everyone; yet my heart was too full of sorrow to be able to see beyond to that. In the kitchen, on the window-sill behind the sink that Julian had recently put in himself, was a jam-jar containing the pussy-willows Bou's children had brought for Father the previous Sunday – the 'pussy-palms' of the countryside. He always had a special love for them, and for Palm Sunday, and we in consequence have shared it. It was a poignant moment when I saw the silvery buds there, on that morning.

I stayed on at Ashcott for some weeks, helping Mother to get her life onto some kind of an even keel. Her leg got better, with time and care; but she had aged a lot. We were all anxious about her being alone in that rather rambling house, particularly at night; but she wanted to stay there. So in the end I came away, but it was with some misgiving.

While in Ashcott I had seen more changes in the village since my previous visit about eight years before. More and more bungalows had sprung up and new roads made where fields had been. In my growing years I can only recall two bungalows in the whole village. Many more of the people I had known, and who had been part of my life for years, were now laid to rest in the quiet churchyard, where we had buried Father's body. I love that Walt Whitman poem where he says that all the people he had known, and all the things he had seen and heard and understood, had become part of him, and he part of them. I felt the truth of this very much when I walked around that little church-yard, and when I heard the church-bells ringing on the Sunday morning. It, they, all were part of me as I was then, and as I am now.

One thing I learned at that time was how important it is to write to people we know when they have suffered a bereavement. Before that, when I was faced with writing such a letter, I had always feared to write it, lest I should put my clumsy foot where angels would fear to tread, and cause even more pain to the dear person to whom I was writing. Often I'd been tempted not to write at all, and hope that my silence would be interpreted as a sensitive respect, or the effect of my having been too deeply saddened to be able to find words. When I saw how much the letters of condolence which Mother received meant to her – though they brought tears – I realised it is far better to write in such cases, even when we can't find words that seem suitable. Frequently, in any case, they are more suitable than we imagine, because we have tried, and thought, and often prayed beforehand. And however clumsy they may be, they show that at least we have attempted, in our poor way, to express our sympathy. For the recipient, at that moment, that is all that's needed.

Mother carried on in the old home for a while, but this was unsatisfactory. There were so many steps up and down to the rooms, and before long she had another fall. It wasn't serious, though she could not get up for some hours. After a lot of agonising, for her and for us all, she moved into a little bungalow further up the hill on which Ashcott is built, and Julian and his family went to live in the old home. They were very near, and could visit her often. The rest of us kept in touch by telephone; and she courageously set about starting her life anew as a widow in unfamiliar surroundings. She had to leave behind many of her well-loved pieces of furniture, gathered so slowly over the years. But Mother was sensible, and knew that now all her family had gone her needs were few, and easily fulfilled. She had her piano, and several music pupils still coming regularly, though about that time her fingers became curled with arthritis, and she was not really able to play any more – at first she could still do a little, but the result of her efforts was so frustrating to her that she realised her beloved Beethoven and Mozart were now no longer possible for her once so nimble fingers. However, she had her television, and watched out for musical programmes, which always gave her great joy.

Her dog, Katy, and Myskin, the long-haired silver and white Persian cat, both of which she and Father had had from puppy and kittenhood, were great companions for her now. She had always had someone to care for; now she still had these two pets to feed and look after. In fact Katy, a very intelligent bitch of no known breed, but with a most loving nature, really helped to look after her. She kept an eye on Mother's every movement, and if she thought her mistress was not very well she would stay close by her all the time, even going to the bathroom with her as if to make sure she was safe. When Mother could no longer get into the bath, or in any way reach to wash her feet, she would sit on the edge of the bed in the early morning and ask Katy to wash them for her. Katy would sit and lick all over her feet and ankles, up to where Mother could reach, with her rough pink tongue. It was one of her regular duties. Once in a way the chiropodist from the Health Service would come, and give the feet a wash with water; or one of the family did the job for her. Those days, Katy had a morning off.

Mother lived alone in the bungalow, with her little garden, which she loved, for about ten years. None of us felt very happy about her being on her own, particularly as she was diabetic, but it was the only way. She was a very independent lady; and all of us were totally committed either to our families or to our monastic communities. Most of the time she managed surprisingly well, with the help of a number of good people. A home help came once a week, and a lady from Street used to come over and do some jobs in the house and garden, bringing fish and chips, which she and Mother much enjoyed for their lunch. The tradesmen always called, and passed the time of day. She knew them all, and they knew her needs. Two days a week she had Meals on Wheels – a wonderful service.

On one occasion Julian brought his little son George, then about two or three years old, to spend the morning with Granny while he and Judy went shopping.

'He can share your Meals on Wheels', he told her, knowing that this was usually ample. It was one of Mother's great gifts that she was so good with children of any age, and they always loved her – she seemed to know just how to talk with them. Many were the surprising little confidences they would elect to share with her. On that morning George and his Granny had a happy time together, playing his favourite games; then at twelve o'clock she told him that they must get the table laid ready for lunch because the Meals on Wheels would soon be arriving. Together they put on the tablecloth, and collected plates and spoons, and George clambered up onto a chair in the adroit way small children have of wriggling up onto the seat on their tummies first and then swivelling round. Then the car drew up at the door, and a lady came in with the piping hot meal in foil dishes, which she set on the table, smiling at Mother's small guest, then hurrying off to her next visit. Mother served up the food onto both their plates, while George watched in grave silence. Then he looked up with a puzzled expression in his big, dark eyes. 'Where are the wheels, Granny?' he asked.

The Refectory at Wood Hall

Hoeing the leeks at Wood Hall

chapter twenty-five

The sycamore buds

Our Carmel at Wood Hall went through a difficult time when the Ecumenical Centre had to close down, for lack of funds, and the big house was put on the market. We had no idea what its new purpose might be, or whether it would prove impracticable for us to remain there. A great deal of heart-searching went on. At one point we thought of moving elsewhere in Yorkshire. Later, there was the possibility of joining forces with another new Carmel that was just being founded. We even began to think about what could be taken with us – I was keen to dig up and replant in the new place at least two of the apple trees from our now so promising orchard. We prayed, discussed, asked advice, agonised over what to do for the best. Gradually we came to the conclusion that we would remain where we were, unless the Centre premises were used for some quite incompatible purpose. This time of uncertainty lasted for several years.

For a short time, while the Centre still belonged to the Diocese, it was used as a reception centre for Vietnamese boat-people. Families were brought there on arrival in England while homes were being found for them. It was a place where they could get some kind of rest and feeling of stability after the terrible trauma they had lived through, many of them for months and even years. Some were able to be reunited with other members of their families. The staff did everything they could to help them re-adjust, and lots of local people gave whatever assistance they were able to offer. Some gave English lessons, some provided clothing, and later utensils, as homes were found for them. It was a moving and humbling experience to witness the courage and cheerfulness of these new neighbours. The little children were beautiful – often they would run up to our front door, and play around.

Eventually the big house became an hotel, and a very quiet one;

so there was no further need for anxiety on that score. The cottages belonging to it, which would in years gone by have been staff dwellings for the stately home, became private houses, and were developed and improved. This made Wood Hall into almost a little hamlet, which was good. The Carmel, the hotel, and the families in the cottages, though not impinging on one another, are mutually supportive in times of need. Sometimes the steep lane to the village and outside world becomes blocked by ice and snow. Once we had a sister who was very ill at such a time, and a man from one of the cottages managed to get out with a four-wheel drive vehicle, and collect medication for her. At other times we have been able to supply or lend items to help the hotel, or one of the families.

Meanwhile, back at Thicket new members had arrived, so the empty cells we had left were filled again. Some of the older sisters died, and were laid to rest in the cemetery there; but even so the Community soon regained the size it had been before we left to found Wood Hall. In time Bridget became the Prioress, so she had a lot of work on her hands. But she had grown into a calm, sensible person with great breadth of mind, a warm heart, and a good sense of humour, so she coped well. She also retained, and still has, a youthfulness and lightness of touch which have helped both her and the other sisters over many a difficult time.

I went to Ashcott again in 1988, when Mother had a bad chest infection, and pnuemonia was feared. Despite her protestations she simply had to have help, if only for a few days. I found her much more frail, and beginning to be forgetful. It was all very worrying. She didn't want to go into a Home and, even if she had wanted it, none of the others would have been happy about it. Then Julian and his wife decided that they would build a 'granny-flat' onto the old house, where she had lived for so many happy years, and until it was ready she should go and live with them, in a bed-sitter on the ground floor.

Julian was a man of many gifts. He designed the extension himself, hired a JCB to level the land, and built with his own hands a lovely two-roomed flat with its own shower and toilet, adjoining the house. A door from his kitchen gave access, but Mother also had her own front door and patch of garden outside it. The whole blended in well with the old house, because he used the same local stone, and pantiled the roof.

I stayed with her only a little while, until she was over the infection, and then Julian took her to his house after I had returned to Yorkshire. He built the extension within a few months; but unfortunately Mother had a fall, crossing the uneven flag-stones of the courtyard, and broke her hip. We all feared she would not recover from the operation; diabetics have extra problems, and she was eighty. However, with good nursing at the hospital she pulled through, and began to walk again with the aid of a zimmer frame. She had always had plenty of pluck, and this hadn't left her.

Not only did she recover from that operation, but within a few months she had a cataract removed from one eye. This had been planned for a long time; her sight had been getting very poor. Reading had always been a life-line for her, far more than the television. Simon had been getting her large-print books from the library, and they had been a great help; but by the time she was eighty even these had become difficult for her to read.

An incident that occurred a year or so before this is illustrative of her spirit, even in frail old age. One of the family had sent her a length of pretty pink material, with the suggestion that it be made into curtains for her bedroom. Mother told me of its arrival during a chat on the phone.

'It's far too pretty to be made into curtains', she said firmly. 'I'm going to make it into a sun-dress! I've never had a sun-dress, and I've often wished I had!' And sure enough, though the stitches were a far cry from her former neat sewing, and I think someone helped her to machine the sides, she made herself a sun-dress. I don't suppose she had much wear out of it; but it gave her pleasure to feel she could still 'run up a garment'.

After the cataract operation she had to wait some time for the new glasses; but even without them she could see a lot better than before. She looked forward to getting them, and ordered a weekly magazine; and she bought two new books – one of them a wild flower book, so that she could improve her knowledge of the local flora. She told me that when her glasses came she was planning to 'put a face on'. She had never worn make-up of any kind. Hers was a clear, pink-and-white complexion that needed no assistance from the chemists. But some of the younger members of the family had persuaded her to buy a lipstick and some other make-up, now that she had recovered, to a certain extent, from two operations. The arrival of the new glasses was to be the signal for the new face to appear.

But it was not to be. Before they had come, early one morning quite unexpectedly she died. So she never wore her make-up. On the evening before she had phoned me, as bright as can be, and we had a good chat. One of the things she said was 'I've spoken to all my children today'. As things turned out, I was so grateful that we had all had that last happy contact with her. Also on that last day Julian had, on the spur of the moment, taken a snapshot of her sitting outside her new little domain, wearing a pretty summer dress and her beads. She loved beads; and Father had always loved to see her wearing them. On the day she died, a little later in the day, Julian dashed into Street and got that photo developed. He slipped a copy into each of four envelopes, and got them straight into the post, so that we each received one on the following morning. It was such a lovely thought.

We had all loved and revered Mother all our lives, as we had Father. Even now we find ourselves doing things, and coping with unexpected situations, as she would have done. She lives on in the daily living of each of our lives, and we treasure the memory of a noble woman and loving mother.

I wasn't able to go down to Somerset for her funeral, but spent the day quietly at Wood Hall, sharing in my heart with those of the family who were there – all, in fact, except Bridget and me. I sat in the woods almost all day long, silently bearing the pain of loss, and praying for them all. The sycamore trees were just opening their leaf-buds, and scattering the little pink sheaths all over the ground, like confetti. Mother would have appreciated this – she always loved pink; and the newly-opened buds spoke to me of new life, and the resurrection. However old we are when we lose a dear parent it is still as hard. The sisters were all very understanding and supportive, and I was grateful for their kindness.

Over the ensuing weeks Mother's bungalow was sold, and the money shared between us. It was a sad day for me when I saw the solicitor's envelope with my letters. Somehow it seemed so final, so crushing. I just didn't want to look inside it, or have anything to do with the contents. Fortunately for me, the situation was eased in that I didn't have to cope with it immediately. In a Community there is always someone at hand whose work it is to attend to the various details of everyday life for the others. Finances were not my area of competency, so I could hand over the envelope until I had been able to come to terms with my present lot.

Later I was very happy to find that Mother's legacy had enabled us to purchase, at long last, a small but very suitable electronic organ for our chapel. She would have greatly approved of this purchase. It also paid to have some roof-lights put in which made the main passage bright and cheerful. It had always been rather dark. A little incident regarding these was not lost on me. The joiners had come to measure up and discuss the job, and then we waited, and waited, and wondered if they ever would come to do the work. Then one day they arrived, and to our surprise got it all done in a day – three lovely big windows; and I noticed that it was the anniversary of my parents' wedding day.

The Community at Wood Hall with Tertullian (1994)

chapter twenty-six

Tertullian

For a good many of my years as a nun I had been involved in the planning and preparation of the meals and bread-making as my main work, though I usually had a few sidelines as well. In the kind of life we lead, each one has to be able to take a share in the various tasks of the house, as occasion demands, often at short notice. In the main it was congenial work, though there were times when it could be very demanding. I enjoyed, and still do, trying out new recipes, and making up my own. With my war-time back-ground, and the remembrance of Mother's thriftiness as she saved and used everything the garden produced, I loved making jams, jellies and pickles with whatever came to hand.

Then I had a complete change when I was given the care of the vegetable garden. This was a new challenge, and great fun. I had looked after the fruit trees for many years, but now I was involved in providing fresh vegetables all the year round for a vegetarian Community. At certain times of the year this can be comparatively easy; but if you want to continue producing baskets of greens and roots through the difficult months you have to plan and sow more than a year in advance. I was fortunate in that Sister Kathleen, who had done this work with great success for the past dozen years or so, was at hand to give advice. However much previous experience one may have had – and again my mind harked back to Father's gardening tuition – a knowledge of the particular soil and situation is vital to successful crop production. Methods that would work well on deep, fertile soil in a sheltered garden would founder miserably on our thin, stony ground with its exposed position.

With gardening, as with cookery – and indeed with living – one is always a learner. I tried all sorts of things, some a great success, others a waste of time except in that I had learned that they wouldn't grow here. Different weathers as each season progresses affect most crops – every year there are some things that do well, and others that scarcely pay their way. I learned to grow plenty of the vital crops, and a few unusual things as an occasional treat for the Sisters. Some of the vegetables would suddenly overwhelm us with their bounty, so that anyone coming to the door would be offered – or begged to take! – courgettes galore, or runner beans, or whatever it was. Most crops could be preserved in some way, but there wasn't always a solution in that direction. It was not until quite recently that we moved into the realm of deep freezers.

Even now we don't have a lot of freezer-space. Most of the storing-crops are still preserved here by the older methods, which really do give better results. All the root crops – carrots, beet-roots, parsnips and swedes – are stored in bins of sand in the garden-shed, and brought out as we need them right through the winter and into April, or even May. Runner beans are salted in large jars; these last until the bean season comes round again and are a great stand-by. Frozen vegetables always seem to me almost flavourless, whereas the ones from the sand-boxes taste just as if one had dug them straight from the ground. In the same way we find fruits bottled in the traditional way much more satisfactory than frozen ones, apart from raspberries, which freeze very well; so we save our freezer-space for these, mainly.

Because we have always grown our crops organically, there were weeds a-plenty. This meant that there were wild flowers around to attract bees and other pollinating insects, which were a bonus. We kept our own bees for many years; and I have seen a lot of lovely butterflies in the course of my everyday work on the land, which we probably shouldn't have had if the garden had been a model of neatness!

Other sisters helped me with the work, especially at the busiest times, and I had a sturdy rotovator for tilling the soil. I tried to take care of my tools. I've always noticed that the really good gardeners love their tools, and treat them with great respect, as trusty friends and helpers. One of our spades was given to us by an old gardener who had used it all his life, and was able to pass it on to us still in prime condition. It had been made many years ago by craftsmen who took pride in their work, and subsequently cherished.

One day as I was walking across the hayfield that runs along the side of the vegetable garden I saw a gleam of something white in the long grass. Thinking it might perhaps be some wild-flower I had not previously noticed, I walked over to see what it was. When I got near enough I could see it was only a piece of paper. I turned away, and began to retrace my steps; but then a little voice inside me whispered 'keep Britain tidy! You could at least pick it up and take it down to the rubbish bin'. So back I went and picked up the scrap of paper. To my surprise, it was a ticket tied to the stub end of a burst balloon. It asked the finder to post the ticket to a certain address. It was evidently a competition or balloon-race of some kind, so I decided to send it off. Weeks passed, and I thought no more about the incident until a parcel arrived for me. It was a personal stereo, the very first we had ever seen, though we had heard about them. The balloon stump I'd found had been the winning entry in the competition, and the lady who had sent it into the air had won a music centre. Mine was the finder's prize. A day or two later I received a letter from the winner, who lived in Huddersfield and had been given our address. She thanked me for taking the trouble to send off the label; and to this day we have corresponded. 'My balloon lady' I call her, and she and her husband have been to see me occasionally. They never tire of telling their friends the tale of how her balloon landed in a monastery garden, so many miles away. For us, the personal stereo was another step into the world of new gadgets. It lasted a good while; and gradually we were given others, by friends and families.

As the years passed, and I began to get older, though still a keen gardener, we looked at the possibility of getting a small tractor, to help with the transporting of heavy loads so that I wouldn't have to do so much with the wheel-barrow; and also as a grass-cutter. We must have talked about it, on and off, for maybe a couple of years, and collected various brochures about every kind of tractor and ride-on mower. I visualised something that could also plough the land; but this turned out not to be practicable. A machine with a powerful enough engine to draw a plough would need to be too large to be manoeuverable in a garden that has some areas cropped all through the year.

We sought advice, and in the end came up with an excellent solution, which stood us in good stead for the next eight years. We bought a new rotovator, one that started up straight away when the rope was pulled – unlike the old one, which by that time had become very difficult to get running – and a lovely little Wheelhorse tractor, second-hand but all the stronger for that, complete with a mower-deck and a bright little trailer.

How I loved this sturdy little 'horse'! We named it Tertullian, after the famous writer of the second century. It happened to arrive here on March 9th, and on that evening there was a reading from Tertullian's works as part of the service in church. Hauling heavy loads now became a pleasure rather than a chore. Winter firewood could be transported even from the lower reaches of the property; and mowing the grass and the woodland paths was now something to look forward to doing.

We had these machines for more than eight years when both of them, and another lightweight rotovator Thicket had given us, were stolen in the night. I feel I am still suffering from bereavement!

During my years as gardener I had the unusual experience for a Carmelite nun of having to do some travelling. Through a chain of circumstances, it fell to my lot to become a member of a small committee working on behalf of the contemplative nuns in this country. This was not very demanding work, but it did entail going to other monasteries now and again for meetings. When I became a nun I had presumed that I would never again see a train. The journey from Exmouth to York had been, as far as could be foreseen, a once only railway trip; but since then I had made those visits home to Somerset.

Now I found myself on Leeds station several times, over the next few years, with my neat little imitation-leather brief-case containing some papers and the few oddments I needed for a night away from home. On one occasion I had to go to London for a meeting, and back on the same day. This really was a remarkable experience!

Sister Joan drove me to Leeds station early in the morning so that I could catch the seven o'clock train. With hindsight, I realise that I needn't have gone so early; but I wasn't at all sure how long it would take me to get from Kings Cross to the meeting, and I wasn't going to risk going all that way and arriving too late. I was armed with my senior citizen railcard, but even with that reduction it was quite costly to get this swift train. The time given on my ticket for arrival in London was 9 a.m. – exactly two hours. Whatever would Dick Turpin have said, I thought, and I pictured him galloping all those miles on horseback.

The train was already at the platform, and the seats filling up with business-men in smart suits, and ladies equally well, though in most cases more comfortably, attired. From the way they boarded the carriage and went straight to their seats I surmised that for most of them this was an everyday occurrence; they were just going to work. Many, as the journey progressed, went along to the dining-car and had breakfast.

I sat in my seat by the window, taking in my surroundings and looking out at the beautiful English countryside as the train gathered speed. It was a May morning, bright and sunny, with the trees in their new green. One of the business-men in a seat near me was talking into a portable phone and jotting things down, oblivious to the beauties of the passing landscape, at any rate on that journey. Perhaps he was just too busy to feel he could spare the time to look.

For me it was a fascinating trip. One of the things I noticed particularly was the number of spires we passed. In my home county of Somerset almost all the old churches had towers. True, there were a few to been seen on this journey; but almost all the churches had these beautiful spires, pointing up into the sky – 'aspiring', as I once heard it called. I began to watch out for them, and found that there was rarely a point on the journey when there wasn't at least one in sight. Whether or not it was because church and praise were so much a part of my everyday life I don't really know, but the sight of all those beautiful, often very old spires brought me a profound sense of peace, and of being on home ground.

In an incredibly short time we were at Kings Cross: London in just two hours. As I got off the train I looked up at the big station clock and it was indeed 9 a.m. All my fellow travellers alighted and hurried along the platform, obviously well accustomed to the routine and paying no attention to anything or anyone as they left the Station. I stood looking around for a few moments before setting off towards the WAY OUT sign. There were a number of pigeons strolling around on the ground, keeping an eye open for any food scraps that might be available. I felt as though I had been met by friends! They looked so unconcerned about the roar of the train engine which was still continuing even though the train had reached its terminus. Engines were roaring on other platforms, and it was all very noisy, but the pigeons were calm, quite unperturbed, and a comforting sight for a countrywoman.

Strangely, I had a feeling of being at home in London. I could remember quite clearly being on these big stations with my parents when I was small, and I walked tall, with confidence. I'd been advised to take a taxi to the meeting, rather than tackle the Underground on my own. So I looked around, and saw a notice that said TAXIS. I made for this, and came to a wooden corral, such as they use for cattle on ranches. A queue of people stood in it, with their suitcases, or briefcases; and there indeed were the London taxis, zooming in round a semicircular arena, each picking up a passenger and gliding off, and being followed immediately by the next. I joined the queue, clutching my neat little leatherette case in one hand, and a plastic bag containing several large sticks of home-grown rhubarb (my speciality!) and a little morning-glory plant in the other. I had brought these as gifts for one of the Sisters at the meeting.

When my turn came I knew exactly what to do, having watched all the others carefully. When the driver pulled down his window I said, 'Mount Street', as if I went in taxis every day. However, I wasn't quite as clever as I'd thought I was, because I fumbled with the door, not having a clue as to how to open it! The driver was a helpful man, and kindly opened it from the inside, so I got in and settled onto the seat, and we, too, zoomed off.

I saw a little of London as we passed through, but not very much. The street names were somehow so familiar. I suppose we see them quite often in advertisements, and books – or perhaps the memories stem from childhood days, and hearing our parents and relatives speaking about them. I admired the way the driver skilfully threaded his way in and out of the many vehicles, bicycles and pedestrians thronging the streets.

It only took a short time, nothing like the hour or more I had been told to expect, to reach Mount Street, where the meeting was to take place. The driver wouldn't take the full fare; he said, 'God bless you, Sister', and pointed out the door at which I must ring before he drove away. His kindness was my introduction to life in London. I don't suppose he had any idea what it had meant to me.

On my return journey I did use the Underground, because one of the other nuns at the meeting was travelling by the same route for the first part of her journey, and she was well accustomed to travelling. Although as a small child I had been on escalators it was a very long time ago; so this was an unusual experience. At the lower end a busker was playing a saxophone, and the music filled the whole vast area, echoing through the tunnels – an unexpected concert!

The sister made sure I was on Kings Cross station before leaving me for her own train, and soon I was on my way up-country in the early evening sunshine. It had been a long and full day, so different from my normal life, and I felt more tired than I would have done if I had been digging and hoeing all day!

Sister Mary, Foundress of Wood Hall Carmel

Bridget and Marie on the occasion of the Silver Jubilee

chapter twenty-seven

The silver jubilee

So much of our everyday life in the monastery wouldn't be of much interest to anyone who hasn't actually experienced a similar kind of life. Obviously, many of the daily joys and sorrows, ups and downs will be just like the ones you meet yourself. We share so many lovely things – the painted lady butterflies this summer, for instance, and the changing garden as the seasons come and go, the bird-song, even the snow piled high against our doors on a January day, and the blessed shelter of a roof – which it is so easy to take for granted. And no doubt you too have to cope with the knocks and blocks and daily rubs, machines that won't start, people who don't turn up when they say they will, and just plain difficult days when even the handles inexplicably fall off the mugs. The threads of all our lives are so closely interwoven that most of us can at least recognise the pattern.

There are times when we are brought to the very edge; but even there we know we are not alone. So many other people, at any time of any day, are there on the brink with us. I think of all those who ask us to pray for them – people in impossible situations, yet apparently living normal lives. A lot of our friends who are also nuns work with the needy and suffering in very many areas, and we can't help trying to carry some of their problems. I don't know how people manage at all if they haven't any faith.

One of the questions people often ask us is 'Isn't your life very monotonous? You seem to do the same things at the same time day after day, year in and year out. You never go away for a holiday, and you don't often meet people other than your own Community'. Well, of course, life just isn't as predictable as that. Sometimes we quite wish we *could* get a day that is straightforward, and on which we are able to do just what we had planned. True, we do have set times for getting up, going to the chapel, and having our meals; but no one can foresee what may happen when plans don't turn out as expected. It takes a lot of work and arranging to keep everything ticking over and the bills paid, just as it does in most people's homes.

It can be pouring with rain on the morning you had expected to be able to plant your potatoes, so you get on with the accounts indoors instead. The next day the sun is shining. 'Potatoes today!' you say to yourself as you pull on your wellies – only to realise that it's Wednesday, and the mechanic is coming at nine o'clock to service some piece of equipment in the house that has been playing up. 'He won't take long', you comfort yourself, knowing that you will have to stay indoors to explain what has been amiss. 'I'll be out by half past nine'. He, however, is stuck in a traffic jam miles away, and won't get to your machine until eleven at the earliest. By the time he has been and gone, the bell for church has rung, and then dinner will be ready. There's no chance of going out later in the day, because your afternoon is fully booked with indoor work. 'Potatoes tomorrow', you tell yourself resignedly. Don't try to tell me that this kind of thing never happens to you!

One morning I had expected to be able to do a cleaning job that has been on my list of things-that-must-be-done for weeks. Just as I was about to begin I received an urgent message from one of the sisters – the drains were blocked! So it was overalls on, drain-rods out, inspection covers up, and that was the end of my morning. Some people would have called in a plumber to do this job; but that would have meant another bill, and probably taken up just as much of our time. We try to do all we can ourselves in the way of maintenance.

Sometimes really lovely things happen, and one just drops tools and enjoys them! Just as there are the very sad days of loss and grief. These are the times when more than at all others we realise the strength and comfort that lies in the presence of the Community. As our joys are shared, and our work and prayer, so also are our sorrows. A kind word – even just a glance – can be a source of untold comfort and support in a time of great suffering and need. 'A faithful friend is a tower of strength', and this is a truth we have all experienced here, in our darker moments. The other old saying that 'a joy shared is a joy doubled, and a sorrow shared is a sorrow halved', is nowhere more manifest than in a Community. Even though, at times, one's suffering may be something quite hidden and known only to oneself, others will sense that one is carrying an extra burden, and will make those gentle allowances that mean so much. A Community is, after all, a family, bound together not by bonds of flesh and blood but by a shared conviction, a common aim, and deep love.

Although we never go away for holidays, we quite often have happy days of celebration at home. There are the big festivals of the calendar – Christmas, of course, and Easter, Whitsun, and other days through the year. And there are anniversaries, jubilees, sometimes a Clothing or Profession ceremony – and even just a 'free day' given for a domestic reason and always enjoyed to the full. All of these provide a welcome change; some are planned and prepared for well in advance, especially if they are to be accompanied by a church service that requires music. Others are more impromptu, and often even more fun in consequence. Simple joys are not lost on us – I think, in fact, that in Carmel we appreciate lots of things much more fully than we would do if we lived elsewhere and had more options at our command. Home-made entertainments are usually the best, and give most pleasure. Some of the plays that Sister Patricia has produced at Christmas-time have been excellent. Sometimes a couple of sisters will organise an entertainment, or do a mime or dance.

Then there is music for pleasure, on occasion. A few of us play recorders; some play guitars, or a keyboard; others have lovely singing voices. Two are very good organists. And others again are not musically inclined, though they enjoy listening.

Some sisters enjoy hobbies, which can be pursued when there's free time on festive days, such as drawing, needle-work, gardening, reading etc. In fact, there's always lots to do, and one has to choose with care how best to use the precious time.

Every week there is Sunday, which is kept as a special day; I always look forward to Sundays. The remunerative work is not done on that day, only the necessary domestic chores; so there is time to be free and choose how it will be spent. It is a more restful day, a welcome refreshment before another busy week begins.

One very special celebration a couple of years ago is of particular interest. The occasion was our Silver Jubilee – the year we celebrated twenty-five years since the founding of Wood Hall Carmel. We wanted this to be a time of thanksgiving, of looking back over the past, and forward to the future. Various projects were planned, each in its own way memorable. For instance, we were allowed to have an open day, so that friends from all around could come in and see the house and garden – something they are not normally permitted to do. This was much appreciated, even though a heavy thunderstorm broke in the middle of the afternoon, so that all the people had to shelter indoors, and the little tables and chairs we'd scattered about the garden looked a pathetic sight.

The two days we shall probably all remember best, however, were in May and October. On 5th May 1994, we all made a historic journey back to Thicket; and then later in the year the Thicket Sisters all came to Wood Hall. All was planned with care and great love. Those of us who had come from Thicket, all those years ago, were longing to see again the house and the Community we had left. The younger sisters, who had joined us during the twenty-five years, were equally keen to see the place of which they had heard so much.

So we all set off, about mid-morning, packed into the cars of various kind friends. By this time we had a car of our own, so this took four of us. Everyone was in great spirits, and we from this end hardly noticed that it was pouring with rain. But the Thicket sisters had planned that much of the day would be spent in their lovely garden, because we'd had beautiful weather for weeks, and had almost forgotten about rain. They had arranged an *al fresco* lunch on the lawn outside their community room, all daintily set out with flowers and pretty serviettes on the tables. It had been overcast to begin with, but dry, so they had carried on with their outdoor preparations. However, not long before we were due to arrive, the rain fell in earnest. The welcoming bunting, so cleverly designed and executed, hung limply against the wall, and the sisters hurriedly rearranged everything indoors.

When we arrived we were greeted with exuberant song, and escorted across the courtyard, under the dripping bunting, and into the Community room. In the few minutes before our arrival they had set out the meal in there, and it all looked so pretty, with little home-made candles in tiny saucers of flowers, that we felt it couldn't possibly have been better. In a way it was a blessing that we were all able to be together – it was a big room, so there was plenty of space, yet each had a chance to greet old friends and meet the new ones.

Despite the rain it was a most happy day. We looked around the house, and later the wet garden when the rain had abated. We prayed together, singing Vespers, – one big Community, so closely united in love and friendship. We visited the two very elderly invalid sisters in the Infirmary wing – later they both came along in their wheel-chairs to share the meal with us.

The day passed all too quickly; but before we left we were each given a little gift-parcel to bring home. Everything had been thought of to make the day joyous and memorable. Bridget was Prioress, and she always had a gift for organising special events – and some willing helpers to aid her in bringing her ideas to fruition.

It was another milestone in the lives of both monasteries. Time had moved on – very visibly in many ways; yet for those few hours it had seemed to stand still. Those of us who had been at Thicket during our formative years as nuns felt that we were back where we began, and the twenty-five years slipped away almost as though they had never been, and were yet to come. There were some very poignant moments, as when I watched Bridget bending tenderly over the old, now invalid, Sister Mary who had been so full of energy and action at the time we left Thicket. Their roles had been reversed. Bridget had at that time been still fairly new in the life, and needed support. Now she herself was the one who carried the heavy burdens of administration and caring for all the various needs of the Community.

Then in October it was we who were the hosts, and everyone – yes, even the most infirm, though they returned home earlier – came from Thicket to Wood Hall. Many of the younger sisters had never seen it. A few had come to see us before joining Thicket, but had only seen the outside, and the extern quarters. We had a beautiful service together in the chapel. To celebrate the Mass we were even able to have with us the Bishop whose inspiration it had been to found the Carmel.

I think many of us were moved to tears as we sang and prayed together, and then shared a meal of thanksgiving in the Community room. Even the two from Thicket who were in wheel-chairs were quite obviously enjoying the day. Though again it was wet, there was so much happiness and sunshine indoors that it didn't matter. Even the tears were tears of joy and gratitude and in no way a damper on the day.

Bridget and I slipped upstairs together with our lunch – it was a kind of buffet which we'd been able to prepare beforehand. We sat in my cell, eating while we talked together of so many things. I watched her as she spoke and ate, and noticed little mannerisms that she had had as a child, and others that I remembered Mother having. She had inherited gifts from both our parents.

We spoke of them, and of the family, now moving into a new generation. And we looked back to the time of the opening of this Carmel, and the people who had been so instrumental in bringing it into being. We remembered in particular the priest who, in his quiet way, had given us encouragement by his vision and under-standing, Father Paul White. He had long since died, but we still have copies of some of his inspired talks, as well as a few of his poems. One never fails to lift my spirit when it begins to flag – so brief, yet containing insights that would take volumes to describe:

> *Jewelled shades*
> *To have seen*
> *Is to have lived.*
> *Enough said.*

It seems to me to epitomise the lives of my family. I like to think that we have all 'seen', even I.

When we rejoined the others, with our empty mugs and paper plates (we had carefully planned that there would be as little washing-up as possible on that day!) they were setting off to explore our house. The garden was very wet, and not its usual inviting self, except to a few totally dedicated garden-lovers, who ventured out in borrowed macs and boots. Everyone wanted to see all they could, so that they could picture us at our work and daily living. Those who had known the original little building, in the days when we used to come over to scrub and paint the new Carmel, could scarcely believe all that had been accomplished. It was good for the young members of both Communities to meet and have the chance of a chat, a thing so rare in our kind of life. It is what we hope may in time be allowed occasionally, in these days of fewer people joining religious orders.

It was 8 p.m. by the time they left for home, though the older ones had returned earlier with their devoted infirmarian. We all adjourned to the kitchen and had a hot bed-time drink before retiring to our cells, our hearts full of gratitude for the beautiful experience of that day. For me it had been even more special, and Bridget and I will long treasure the memory of sitting together and sharing our deepest thoughts.

chapter twenty-eight

Sunset over the hill

Someone once told me that as we get older many things come round full circle, and we begin to see how apparently disparate things in our lives really fit together. I can't say that this has happened to me – maybe I am not quite old enough yet. And yet, a few occasions have taken me by surprise as they flick me back in thought into a time I had considered long gone. For instance, two friends I hadn't seen for nearly fifty years have visited me here within the past few months. They had been part of my life in the days at the Glastonbury school, and I realised that they still continued to be so. How very often that Walt Whitman poem springs to my mind!

Another 'coming round' – or is it 'moving on'? – that happened to me about a year ago was the changing back of my name as a nun from Elizabeth to Marie. A new young sister had joined our Community named Elizabeth. She loved her name; and as she was just starting out on her life in Carmel, it seemed to me a good idea if I slipped back to my old, baptismal name so that she would be able to keep hers. We couldn't very well have two people with the same name; it would have been muddling for everyone, especially for her and for me.

Perhaps the writing down of these reminiscences has in its way been a beginning again from where we set out. When we were children at Ashcott, fired by reading stories of the lives and exploits of other children, I was frequently employed during quieter moments in writing, amongst other things, what I thought of as my memoirs. The games we played, in the garden and surrounding countryside, all appeared to me to be so wonderful and so real that I felt I wanted to record them, and that other children would like to know about them. The fact that many of them were almost entirely imaginary was unimportant to me. There is a kind of 'realness' in a child's world that can rarely be recaptured by adults; a place where make-believe has its roots. Indeed, a child can be hurt and bewildered by his or her 'games' being dismissed as pretence – I have known it happen. Mercifully our own parents were far more perceptive. Even if they couldn't quite grasp what we meant, they knew we could, and respected our secret world.

Many were the beginnings, the 'first chapters' of that narrative that Mother used to find around the house; but as with all we write when we are young, I would discover a few weeks after doing the writing that I had outgrown it. So I would begin again, according to my present capabilities, only to find later that the same thing had happened. Children's minds develop very fast. I suppose our minds continue to develop all our lives, as new experiences teach us more; but not at that speed. We tend to sift, and to filter things as we get older – sometimes too much, so that it is possible to reject new knowledge, which is a great pity. Probably I shall cringe in a year or two when I read what I have written here. I used to call our family 'Linton' when I wrote about it; I was under the impression that when one wrote about people it was the correct thing to do to change the names. I hope this is not so, because I haven't changed any in this book. By coincidence, I have lived at the edge of the Yorkshire village of Linton for the last and longest part of my life.

The idea of writing the book faded entirely from my mind once I began teaching, and subsequently became a nun. Life was by then very full; and in any case in the earlier part I can't imagine that it would have met with approbation. At that time writing was not looked upon as a very suitable occupation for nuns – though in bygone days many of the greatest women writers were nuns, or anchoresses. Over the years it was sometimes suggested that I wrote a book on cookery, or a garden book. I would have quite enjoyed doing so, because I am happy with a pen in my hand, but in fact there hasn't really ever been leisure for such a purpose. In a fairly small Community it takes all our time to earn our living and care for the house and garden and one another during the hours allotted to work. The time we spend in prayer and praise is always zealously guarded, and never encroached upon. Each day, long periods of silent adoration give the space and tranquillity so necessary in this kind of life.

In recent years, both in my own mind and when I've been in contact with the family, the idea of jotting down some of the memories we share has come to the surface again, fleetingly. But it has always been the same story: I'll do it when there's a bit more time. Then one day, suddenly, I came to the realisation that I was approaching my seventies, and that my days were still as full – in fact, more so, because I was getting to a stage when I could no longer burn an occasional candle at both ends without regretting it for days afterwards. In other words, there never would be time. If I were to write, it would have to be done in little bits, a page here, a paragraph there, a fortnight with nothing done maybe, then another page – perhaps while the jam-pan was boiling, or in some odd few moments between other jobs. Nuns don't retire, so it was no use whatever thinking of postponing the work until retirement; and with the years passing by I was not to know how long it would be before I had perhaps lost all memory of the past.

So, one evening, I began to write. I had always been accustomed to fitting in odd jobs in odd minutes. I once read of an American writer who used to add a little more to her latest book whilst her car was stuck in a traffic jam – this was rather encouraging, though I didn't feel that I could get to that point of dedication. It sounds a little too rushed, anyway. In the evenings we get some free time, but quite often I find I have a letter that needs to be answered, or some other homely task that I must do. Again, sometimes I am just so tired by then that I find myself unable to concentrate at all, even on something I enjoy doing so much, and waste precious minutes re-reading the information on the back of an exercise book.

But every now and then we all get a holiday-day, and I can sit out in the woods with my writing-book on my lap just as I used to sit with Bou under the apple trees at Ashcott all those years ago, as a child, scribbling away and watching apple-blossom petals falling onto blades of grass and becoming pierced through by them.

Then came the boost I so needed. My sister-in-law, Simon's wife, wrote one day and said that she would be delighted to type out the manuscript if I really *did* write the book. 'Even if you only did a page a day, it would eventually be done', she wrote. Well, of course, there have been many days when not a word has been written; but all the same the first exercise book began to fill up, and I felt it was a milestone passed when I sent it off to her.

Others of the family then began to give me great encouragement. I knew there would not be time to write a careful, planned account in beautiful English, though that is what I should have liked to do. If it was to be done at all, I would simply have to write 'off the cuff', as the memories came to mind, and accept with humility whatever criticism came my way, as well as my own sense of its lack of polish. At least I'd have had a shot at doing it. Someone whose opinion I greatly value once said to me: 'If a job is worth doing, it's worth doing badly – have you ever thought of that?' I can't now recall what occasioned the remark, but I have often consoled myself with the idea. So many times since then I have been doing some piece of work that I should have so loved to spend time on, and do really perfectly; but the time, and sometimes the wherewithal, has not been available, and I've had to content myself with producing what to my eyes was less than my best.

As the work of writing progressed, so did the idea that other people as well as the family and the Community here might be interested to read the book.

I am growing older now; the energy of earlier days has mostly slipped away, except for little occasional unexpected moments of youthful vigour, brief as an April shower, swiftly come and gone yet bringing refreshment. I'm getting rather deaf; but with a little National Health assistance I can still hear the cry of the curlew as it rises from the bank of the River Wharfe on a May morning, and wings its way high above the garden. The robin's song, and the chiff-chaff in summer with its monotonous little voice that somehow always seems full of enthusiasm – all the wild birds still give me great joy. I hope I shall be able to hear them for a little longer; but even if I can't, I'll still know their music in my heart.

I still know where to look for the first celandine in spring, and which part of the woods the wood-anemones will clothe the earliest. These are things we share; they go right to our roots, and are part of our lives. I sometimes see wild swans fly over, and remember the ones that nest beside the rhines on the moors of Somerset. I feel akin to them, and love to watch the sweep of their strong wings. I can still see quite well, thank God, and am able to appreciate, more than ever before, the wonders of the ever-changing world of nature around me. People say to me: 'Isn't it dull, staying always in one place? You must know every stick and stone'. But of course nature isn't like that – every day it is new, every day there is more to discover, to explore, to gaze upon with amazement and wonder. Even the longest, strongest life-time would be far too brief to allow one to lift more than a tiny corner of the veil and see the exciting treasures hidden in one patch of garden or woodland – not to mention the wild creatures that pass through it, or the wonders of the skies above.

Then there is the endless surprise of people! We think we know those we live with very well indeed – too well, we sometimes feel. We can predict their every word and reaction, or imagine we can; and then, all of a sudden, we see an entirely new side to them, or rather a new depth, and in a way they become new to us. We think 'I *really* know her', but we have in reality seen only another of the limitless number of facets of the 'immortal diamond' that every person is. Often the getting to know, and even more the getting known, are painful moments; but there is no living in love without suffering. To love and to give are synonymous, or so it seems to me; somehow, love must give. The greater the love, the greater the giving, and therefore the greater the joy and happiness, however great the pain. I am sure that this is true in every walk of life. It is certainly so in a religious community, where there is no need to hide or to pretend, but each one is free to be real. There have been times, over the years, when I have thought maybe I was just too sensitive for this kind of life; but mercifully commonsense and grace have prevailed, and I have realised that I would be exactly the same in any other situation – probably more so, without the support and understanding of the others.

Even the external surroundings in a place like this are conducive to a simplified attitude to life. The seasons and weather impinge far more directly when one lives close to them. I often think how much people miss when they can buy fruit and vegetables from supermarkets at almost any season of the year. Gone, for them, the pleasure of the first dish of early peas in June, or the first ripe tomato in July. A surprising number of adults have no idea what is harvested when, even in their own country. To me this seems an impoverishment; but perhaps they wouldn't see it so.

In one of the earlier chapters I mentioned how the reading of the life of St Thérèse of Lisieux when I was a little girl had had such a profound influence on my whole future. I wanted to use my life to the utmost for God and for people everywhere, and it was her example that led me to choose Carmel as the best place for me to attempt this. By coincidence, this year, as I write, celebrations are taking place all over the world in honour of the centenary of the death of this young, quiet Carmelite – who, incidentally and almost unintentionally, wrote a book. We live in a world of seeking out anniversaries to celebrate. Thérèse's book has been translated into numberless languages, and she is known throughout the world, so her centenary year will be one of great rejoicing everywhere. It seems fitting, to me, that I should finish off my book of memories in this year, because I feel I owe her so much. Perhaps she will receive it as a small token of gratitude.

Unlike most of what has gone before, these last pages have been written consecutively as I sat in the garden on a lovely quiet Sunday afternoon. It is time now to put away my pen, and make my way across the orchard and back to the house. I shall walk along beside the hawthorn hedge, where, to my delight, despite the alkalinity of our soil, a solitary clump of sorrel grows.